Prisoners' Deaths in
Local Jails

Prisoners' Deaths in Local Jails

✦

Factors Influencing Inmate Suicide

LISA NIKOL NEALY

iUniverse, Inc.
New York Lincoln Shanghai

Prisoners' Deaths in Local Jails
Factors Influencing Inmate Suicide

iUniverse, Inc.

For information address:
iUniverse, Inc.
2021 Pine Lake Road, Suite 100
Lincoln, NE 68512
www.iuniverse.com

ISBN: 0-595-29312-3

Printed in the United States of America

A Thesis

Submitted to the Graduate School
Jackson State University
in Partial Fulfillment of the Requirements
for the Degree of

MASTER OF ARTS

May 1995

Major Subject: Political Science

I dedicate this study to my outstanding and loving family, especially mom, and am most grateful to God.

Also, I would like to dedicate this book to the families who loved ones were incarcerated in Mississippi jails from 1987-to current whose deaths were ruled "suicide".

PRISONER'S DEATHS IN LOCAL JAILS:
FACTORS INFLUENCING INMATE SUICIDE

A Thesis
by

Lisa N. Nealy

Approved by:

_____ _____
Major Adviser and Chairman   Member

_____ _____
Member   Dean, Graduate School

May 1995

Contents

List of Illustrations

List of Tables

ACKNOWLEDGEMENTS

There are always people who extend their assistance in helping the researcher in every possible way. To these people I extend my thanks: Dr. Calvin M. Miller, Professor and Thesis Advisor, Department of Political Science, Jackson State University: Dr. Mary Coleman, Acting Chair, Department of Political Science, Jackson State University; Dr. Leslie Burl McLemore, Coordinator of Masters Program, Department of Political Science, Jackson State University; Mr. Len Jefferson, Instructor and Computer Lab Technician, Department of Political Science, Jackson State University; Dr. David Swinton, President, Benedict College, Columbia, South Carolina; Dr. Robert Hairston, Jr., Assistant Professor, Department of Economics, Finance and General Business, Jackson State University; Dr. Gene Young, Professor and Civil Rights Activist, Jackson State University and Civil Rights Activist; Mr. Larry Belton, Assistant Director of Recruitment, Jackson State University; and Dr. Orville Cunningham, Professor, Department of Sociology, Jackson State University.

I also want to thank members of my family for their unfettered support who graciously extended their assistance during the early stages of this research. My mom for her nurturing and constant support who photocopied 263 surveys for the new chapter5. My father, Mr. Eddie Earl Nealy, also extended his support by ensuring my safety, he accompanied me to the various jail populations in 1993. Mrs. Maria LouiseNealy-Houston, my sister, accompanied me to jail population in 1993 as my personal assistant and helped distributed the surveys to the inmates. My sisters, Ms. Angel Nealy, and Ms. Tammie Lorene Nealy provided their assistance with survey collation and transportation to jail populations in 1999. I would like to thank my aunt, Ms. Elouise Pringle and my first cousin-brother, Mr. Timothy Anderson for their moral support.

I would be remiss if I didn't recognize those individuals who provided critical comments to Chapter5. Dr. Donn G. Davis, Associate Professor of Political Science and Graduate Director of the Political Science Department at Howard University. I would like to extend my gratitude to the following academic mentors: Dr. Abdul Karim Bangura, Adjunct Professor at Howard University and Assistant Professor of Political Science who is a Researcher-In-Residence at American University in Washington, DC; Dr. Donn G. Davis, Associate Professor of Political Science and Pre-Law Advisor at Howard University in Washington, DC; and Mr. Khalil Abdullah, Executive Director of the National Black Caucus of State Legislators(NBCSL) in Washington, DC.

Also, I would like to thank those people who granted me interviews in 1993: Mr. Dennis Sweet, Attorney at Law, Jackson, Mississippi; Mr. Chokwe Lumumba, Attorney at Law, Jackson, Mississippi; Mrs. Esther Quinn X, former President, Jackson Chapter of the National Association for the Advancement of Colored People; Mr. Frank Blunston, Director, Youth Detention Center, Jackson, Mississippi; Mr. Malcolm E. MacMillan, Sheriff, Hinds County, Mississippi; Mr. W. D. Sollie, Chief of Police, Meridian, Mississippi, and Mr. Thomas R. Mayfield, Assistant District Attorney, Jackson, Mississippi.

These individuals were contacted for a post face-to-face interview in 1999, but most of thses people had either moved, relocated, or phone numbers were unlisted. Therefore, only one of these individuals had not relocated, Sheriff Malcolm E. MacMillian.

ABSTRACT

Prisoners' Deaths in Local Jails: Factors Influencing Inmate Suicide

May 1995

by

Lisa Nikol Nealy

B.A.

Jackson State University

Advisor: Dr. Calvin M. Miller

This study is designed to ascertain the factors that led to suicide among jail and prison inmates in the state of Mississippi. The sample population for this study was derived from 143 inmates in three jails in the State of Mississippi, and was composed of black, white and Hispanic inmates. The major hypothesis for this research is that suicide is more likely to occur in jails where there is an increase of overcrowding, isolation and deplorable conditions. Discriminate analysis was the sampling method used to ascertain the information on the relationship and association between overcrowding, deplorable conditions and isolation, coupled with predictor variables and their association among inmates who have attempted suicide.

The canonical correlation and Wilks-Lambda was used to demonstrate and analyze the responses that were measured at the .05 level or probability. Hypotheses 1, 2 and 3 were rejected because there was not a statistically significant relationship between attempted suicide, overcrowding, deplorable conditions and isolation. However, predictor variables, such as drug abuse, alcohol abuse, those awaiting trial, offense charged with, self-esteem, parents perception, were accepted because there existed a statistically significant relationship between attempted suicide and these minor variables.

The findings showed that an inmate's self-esteem and the perception of the family were greater factors that contributed to inmate suicides other than over-crowding, deplorable conditions and isolation. Despite these physical conditions in a jail, the findings showed that an inmate is susceptible to suicide when he suffers from low self-esteem and when his family cares very little about him.

Based on these findings, my research hypothesis 1, overcrowding, contributed to prison and jail inmate suicides; hypotheses 2, deplorable conditions, contributed to prison and jail inmate suicides; and hypotheses 3, isolation, contributed to prison and jail inmate suicides were rejected because their levels of significance were higher than .05.

PREFACE

Since 1987, there have been 49 inmate deaths in jails and prisons across the state of Mississippi. We have heard about the recent deaths of inmates in the local jails on television or have read in newspaper about these tragic deaths that have occurred in Mississippi. For instance, Andre Jones, an 18-year-old black male, was found hanging by his shoelace in the Simpson County Jail. Bobby Everett, a 19-year-old black male was found hanging in his Hinds County jail cell. Cedric Walker, a 23-year-old black male, was found hanging in a Parchman prison cell with his larynx and muscles missing. David Scott Campbell, an 18-year-old black male was found hanging in his jail cell in Neshoba County with his tongue cut out and body covered with bruises. These were only a few such events which have been reported on television, the radio, and newspapers.

My main objective in this research is to explore possible reasons why detainees and prisoners are allegedly committing suicide or who have thought about suicide, and if not suicide, why they are being hung. Finally, this research will try to open the eyes of those white Anglo-Saxon Americans, whose conceptual view is that these jail incidents are black victims and not white. Wrong, 24 of the 49 inmates who have died were white. So, this issue concerns not only black, but whites as well. Thus, the extent of this study heightens the discussion of suicides in local jails across the state of Mississippi.

1

INTRODUCTION

What is suicide? Suicide is death resulting from behavior that the individual knows will lead to his own demise.[1] The suicidal act may be positive (entailing some expenditure of energy) or negative (entailing the conscious refusal to take necessary actions for survival)[2]. Suicide has generally been understood as the intentional taking of one's own life.[3] Also, suicide is an act of revenge, an escape from humiliation, or a communicator.[4]

Suicide is deficient in social interest; that is, defacing in social interest is a common factor in all disturbed people (neurotics, psychotics, addicts, and criminals).[5] Suicide is often an act of aggression against others.[6] Further, suicidal people will have developed feelings of inferiority and low self-esteem.[7] Suicide is the same as "homicide" except that the victim is the "self".[8] It also is an escape from an intolerable life situation.[9]

Suicide came to be regarded as taboo within the religious tradition.[10] In 1917, a New Jersey Court declared that an attempted suicide was an indictable offense punished by imprisonment not exceeding three years and a fine not more than

1.   Whitney Pope <u>Durkheim's Suicide: A Classical Analysis</u> (Chicago, Illinois: The University Press, 1978), 10.
2.   Ibid.
3.   Ibid., 11.
4.   David Lester <u>Suicide From a Psychological Perspective</u> (Springfield, Illinois: Charles C. Thomas, 1988), 9.
5.   Ibid., 84.
6.   Ibid.
7.   Ibid.
8.   Atkinson J. Maxwell <u>Discovering Suicide: Studying in the Social Organization of Sudden Death</u> (Pittsburgh, Pennsylvania: University of Pittsburgh Press, 1978), 89.
9.   Karl A. Menninger <u>Man Against Himself</u> (New York, New York: Harcourt, Brace and World, Inc., 1938), 17.
10. Earl A. Ggrollan <u>Suicide</u> (Boston Massachusetts: Beacon Press, 1988), 15.

$1,000 or both.[11] Thirty-five years later, a New Jersey statute terminated possible prosecution for attempted suicides.[12] During this time, South Carolina, Alabama, and Massachusetts considered attempted suicide to be a crime, but of course, not punishable if accomplished.[13]

Suicide reached its greatest proportion in Japan, where it was embedded in religious and national tradition.[14] Suicide was a form of punishment meted out only to offenders of noble birth. They could expiate their crimes and "save face" by dying at their own hands rather than by the sword of the public executioner.[15] Suicide is an act of sadness and desperation when the pattern of life becomes too rigorous or exact and cannot adopt itself; the forces of death take over.[16]

The present research seeks to answer the following questions: (1) Does overcrowding in jails cause an inmate to commit suicide? (2) Does isolation in jails cause inmates to commit suicide? And (3) Do deplorable conditions within jail cells cause an inmate to commit suicide?

The term suicide is defined as any person who voluntarily takes his own life because of unhappiness and the loss of compassion to live. Hence, the term suicide has been modified with Dennis L. Peck. Also, suicide is a major cause of detention deaths, and the legal responsibilities associated with detainee custody are of concern to the law enforcement community.[17] State action against police officers involving detainee suicide takes the form of wrongful death or negligence claims based on tort law.[18]

In particular, State Courts generally recognized that law enforcement officials had a duty to care for persons in their custody.[19] This meant that police had a legal responsibility to take reasonable precautions to ensure the health and safety of persons in their custody; they had to keep a detainee from harm, render medical assistance when necessary and treat detainees humanly.[20]

---

11. Ibid., 16.
12. Ibid.
13. Ibid.
14. Ibid., 23.
15. Ibid.
16. Dennis L. Peck Fatalistic Suicide (Palo Alto, California: R and E Research Associates, Inc., 1979), 16.
17. Police Chief Journal (Volume LVIII, No. 8, August 1991), 53-59.
18. Ibid.
19. Ibid.
20. Ibid.

LITERATURE REVIEW

There is a wealth of literature on suicides in jails and prisons: some of the most important literature includes works done by Neil P. Cohen and James J. Gober, Rights of Prisoners; Gregory E. Winkler, Community Mental Health Journal; David Lester, Suicide From a Psychological Perspective; Alison Liebling, Suicides in Prison; Jay S. Albanse, Federal Probation: A Journal of Correctional Philosophy and Practice; and Whitney Pope, Durkheim's Suicide: A Classical Analysis.

Why are these works prominent in prison and jail suicide literature? These works are important because each of these authors have made an enormous contribution in the study of prison and jail suicides. Each of these works has shown that the most important factors which influence an inmate committing suicide are isolation, overcrowding, and deplorable conditions within the cells.

What themes emerged from the literature? Are the themes time centered or did similar themes appear in periods covered throughout the literature? Most of all, did these themes differ on factors influencing inmates to commit suicide, and how if at all, have these themes changed over time?

Where do most suicides occur? According to Thomas L. Winfre, who has written several published articles on jail inmate suicide which included "Toward Understanding State-Level Jail Mortality," Justice Quarterly, 1987, "Rethinking Americas Jail Death 6 Rates," Policy Studies Review, 1988, and is the co-author of an article entitled, "An Aggregate Level Study of Inmates Suicides and Deaths Due to Natural Causes in U.S. Jails," Winfre stated in David Lester's study that most suicides in American jails.[21] R. Frost and R. Hanzlich who co-authored a book entitled, "Deaths in Custody" and have done studies on jail suicides, found that 26 percent of deaths in a county jail were from suicide, and all were from hanging.[22] H. Hoff, who has conducted several studies on inmate suicide and is the author of "Prevention of Suicide Among Prisoners" published in Jailhouse Blues 1973, found higher rates of both completed and attempted suicides occurred in prisons than in the general population, with hanging and jumping used most by completers and cutting by attempters.[23]

Jay Albanese's view seemed compatible with Winfre, Frost, and Hoff's view on prison and jail high suicide rates. Albanese indicated that suicides were far more common in jails and prisons than they were on the outside.[24] There is

---

21. David Lester Why People Kill Themselves (Springfield, Illinois: Charles C. Thomas Publishers, 1992), 113.

22. Ibid.

23. Ibid., 112.

agreement among investigators that a high percentage of those who have died from self-inflicted wounds either had a history of self-destructive behavior, or had clearly manifested their intentions to do so before accomplishing the act.[25] In addition, Earl Grollman indicated that the incidence of suicide in short-term lock-ups such as municipal jails was nearly five times that of the general population and nearly six times that in long-term prisons.[26] Grollman indicated that everyone placed in cell was at a higher potential suicide risk.[27]

Overcrowding in jail and prisons emerged as the second theme from the literature. According to Wooldredge and Winfre, the higher degree of crowding corresponded with greater numbers of inmate suicide and natural deaths.[28] Likewise, Malcolm MacMillan indicated that the jails in Mississippi were too overcrowded.[29]

Neil Cohen and James Gobert indicated that the courts showed greater agreement on the fact that overcrowded conditions violated the Eighth Amendment of inmates.[30] Moreover, the plight of pre-trial detainee living in overcrowded conditions was an act least one respected noted by the Court, markedly different from that of convicted prisoners. For instance, pre-trial detainees were exposed to overcrowded conditions for a finite period; prisoners generally faced the far longer exposure tot he challenged conditions.[31]

Alison Liebling's view seemed compatible with the views of Cohen and Mac-Millan on overcrowding. Liebling indicated that overcrowding in prisons was often linked in some way to suicide.[32] For example, rates of illness complaints,

---

24. Jay S. Albanese, "Preventing Inmate Suicide", <u>Federal Probation: A Journal of Correctional Philosophy and Practice</u> Volume 47 (March 1983): 65.

25. Ibid., 65.

26. Grollman, 57.

27. Ibid.

28. John Wooldredge and Thomas Winfre, "An Aggregate Level Study of Inmate Suicides and Deaths Due to Natural Causes in U.S. Jails", <u>Journal of Research in Crime and Delinquency</u> (November 1992): 467.

29. Malcolm E. MacMillan, Sheriff of Hinds County, interview by Lisa Nikol Nealy, 21 October 1993, Jackson, Mississippi, Personal.

30. Neil Cohen and James Gobert <u>Rights of Prisoners</u> (Colorado Springs, Colorado: Shepard's and McGraw-Hill, 1981), The Eighth Amendment prohibits cruel and unusual punishment, 308.

31. Ibid.

32. Alison Liebling <u>Suicides inPrison</u> (New Fetter Lame, London: Routelege, Chapman and Hall, Inc., 1992), 52.

levels of psychological stress and death rates have been found to be disproportionately high in overcrowded prisons.[33]

Isolation of inmates emerged as another theme from the literature. Gregory Winkler indicated that isolation increased the risk of suicide among inmates.[34] Placing an inmate alone in a cell occurs in a jail for different reasons including protection of the inmate and others.[35] Grollman indicated that it was isolation within the cell that contributed tot he high occurrence of lock-up to suicides.[36]

John Palmer indicated that the physical state of a cell was another aspect of the conditions of isolation confinement.[37] In illustration, the existence of certain conditions in cells has led to varying results. First, the confinement of more than two men in a single cell in punitive isolation or administrative segregation was unconstitutional in non-emergency situations.[38]

In particular, punitive isolation was ruled unconstitutional for isolating an inmate of more than 15 days.[39] In this type of isolation, an inmate is punished for specific actions. Administrative isolation indicated that an inmate was punished for more severe behavioral problems for longer periods.[40] However, the courts indicated that those inmates on death row could not be isolated inn their cells for long periods of time without outdoor exercise.[41]

Deplorable conditions emerged as another theme from the literature. As early as 1978, charges against the state's jails called many of them inhumane, depriving prisoners of their constitutional rights.[42] Specifically, 11 witnesses, including six inmates, testified at the time of 19-year-old Bobby Everett's alleged suicide, that city jails were filthy and detention officers routinely ignored requests for simple necessities, such as toothpaste.[43]

---

33. Ibid.
34. Gregory Winkler, "Assessing and Responding to Suicidal Jail Inmates," Community Mental Health Journal (August 1992): 320.
35. Ibid.
36. Grollman, 57.
37. John Palmer Constitutional Rights of Prisoners (Columbus, Ohio: The W.H. Anderson Company, 1973), 58.
38. Ibid.
39. Ibid.
40. Ibid.
41. Ibid.
42. Charles Tisdale, "Focus of Feds Investigation Into Suicide Questions," Jackson Advocate (May 20-27, 1993), 1A.
43. Ibid.

Later, one of the witnesses, a health inspector, declared that kitchen facilities were so unsanitary that no hot water was available for kitchen workers to wash their hands.[44] Also, Wooldredge and Winfree indicated that inmate suicides and natural deaths might have occurred less often in jails with more humane conditions of confinement.[45] These environments might be less stressful to inmates, as a result, reducing the number of attempted suicides.[46]

Accordingly, during testimony in 1980, Hickerson Smith, a psychiatrist, indicated that cramped cell conditions and lack of outdoor recreation and direct light lowered self-esteem.[47] Smith also indicated that inmates who had been forced to consume meals in close proximity to toilets provoked feelings of anger and disgust.[48] Thomas Mayfield, who is the Assistant District Attorney in Hinds County, indicated that jails were a depressive and stressful environment for inmates to live. Mayfield indicated that this type of environment provoked inmate suicides.[49]Mayfield stated that a jailhouse was not a pleasant place to be confined, and that some people handled it very well locked up, others do not.[50]

Esther Quinn X, whose 18-year old son, Andre Jones, allegedly committed suicide in the Simpson County Jail, indicated that the conditions of most jails in Mississippi was such that an inmate could be brought to suffer emotional and psychological harm.[51] Frank Blunston indicated that a lot of stress and frustration of inmates due to horrible conditions in the jails created a low-self-esteem, loss of self control which led to suicide.[52]

On the contrary, the Courts view varied on the issue of deplorable conditions in jails and prisons. For example, one Court found that a lack of water and a

---

44. Ibid.

45. John Wooldredge and Thomas Winfree, "An Aggregate-Level Study of Inmates Suicides and Deaths Due to Natural Causes in U.S. Jails," Journal of Research in Crime and Delinquency, (November 1992) : 467.

46. Ibid.

47. Charles Tisdale, "Feds Look Into City Jail Conditions," Jackson Advocate (July 1993): 1A.

48. Ibid.

49. Thomas Mayfield, Assistant District Attorney, interview by Lisa Nikol Nealy, 26 October 1993, Jackson, Mississippi, Personal.

50. Ibid.

51. Esther Quinn X, Former President of Jackson Chapter of National Association for the Advancement of Colored People, interview by Lisa Nikol Nealy, 8 November 1993, Jackson, Mississippi, Personal.

52. Frank Blunston, Director of Detention Center, interview by Lisa Nikol Nealy, 26 October 1993, Jackson, Mississippi, Personal.

shower provided every fifth day did not constitute unhygienic conditions.[53] The Court also stated that the deprivation of a comb, pillow, toothpaste, and toothbrush for 7-10 days in a maximum-security cell did not constitute deplorable conditions or cruel and unusual punishment.[54]

The lack of trained staff emerged as another theme from the literature. According to Representatives of the United States Justice Department, who examined the conditions in Jackson city jails indicated that Mississippi was one of the few states with no standards for jail inspections, and that the state did not require jailers to have any training.[55]

Malcolm E. MacMillan, Hinds County Sheriff, indicated that one of the factors that contributed to inmate suicides and deaths was a lack of adequate supervision.[56] For example, the death of Timothy Lindsey resulted when a jailer failed to check on the suicidal inmate.[57] Particularly, a jailer was supposed to have checked on Lindsey every few minutes because he was considered a suicidal risk. However, the jailer did not check on Lindsey, as a result, Lindsey committed suicide.[58]

Herman indicated that any time an inmate hints at suicide, the inmate should be checked on every five to ten minutes.[59] In addition, Dennis Sweet, who was the attorney for the witnesses who testified before the panel on human rights about conditions in Mississippi jails, indicated that the police committed some of the Mississippi hangings.[60]

Nevertheless, racism emerged as another theme from the literature. Andre Jones, a black Mississippian, was found hanged by his shoelace in the Simpson County Jail.[61] Jones was the 42nd inmate to die by hanging in state jails since 1987. The death of Jones was still ruled a suicide by a local coroner.[62]

---

53. Palmer, 58.
54. Ibid.
55. Tisdale, 1A.
56. Malcolm E. MacMillan, Sheriff of Hinds County, interview by Lisa Nikol Nealy, 21 October 1993, Jackson, Mississippi, Personal.
57. C.L. Thornton, "City Jail Prisoner Apparently Keeping Promise to Kill Himself," Clarion-Ledger (Tuesday, May 25, 1993), 1A.
58. Ibid.
59. Ibid.
60. Dennis Sweet, Attorney, interview by Lisa Nikol Nealy, 13 October 1993, Jackson, Mississippi, Personal.
61. Mark Mayfield and Tom Watson, "Jail Deaths Spark Call for Probe," USA Today (February 19, 1993): 3A.
62. Ibid.

According to pathologist Jame Bryant, someone in the jail killed Jones, and whoever killed him took the body and hung it up to make it look like a suicide.[63] United States Civil Rights Commission Chairman, Arthur Fletcher, indicated that racism played a part in the Mississippi jail incidents.[64] Fletcher also pointed out that there was a pattern of going to jail in Mississippi and being hanged.[65]

Chokwe Lumumba, who represented the Jones Family in a lawsuit against Simpson County, indicated that the alleged suicides of black males were a kind of Old fashion lynching.[66] Lumumba also indicated that hangings reflected the backwardness of Mississippi jails.[67]

The death of 23 year-old Cedric Walker was racially motivated.[68] Walker's body was found hanging in Parchman prison on July 18, by guards.[69] According to Eckert, the pathologist for the family indicated Walker's larynx and throat muscles were missing.[70] Eckert concluded that this made Walker's death impossible of suicide.[71]

The death of 21 year-old David Scott Campbell was racially motivated. Campbell was found hanged by his jeans in the Neshoba County Jail on October 10, 1990.[72] Campbell's father indicated that the police department killed his son because he dated a white girl.[73] Also, Neil Griffin, the girlfriend of Campbell, overheard Neshoba County Sheriff Glen Waldale saying he did not care what happened to black people.[74]

Bobby Everett's death was racially motivated. Everett, 19-years-old, was held on armed robbery and automobile theft charges.[75] Although arresting officers

---

63. Ibid.
64. Ibid.
65. Ibid.
66. Chokwe Lumumba, Attorney, interview by Lisa Nikol Nealy, 14 October 1993, Jacskon, Mississippi, Personal.
67. Ibid.
68. Charles Tisdale, "Autopsy on Hanging Victim Raises New Questions," <u>Jackson Advocate</u> (July-August 1993): 1A.
69. Ibid.
70. Ibid.
71. Ibid.
72. Tom Roster, "Families Tell Panel of Jail Deaths," <u>Clarion-Ledger</u>, (March 18, 1993): 1A.
73. Ibid.
74. Ibid.
75. Charles Tisdale, "Brother Says Suicidal Victim Routinely Beaten," <u>Jackson Advocate</u> (February-March 1993): 1A.

found no evidence that linked Everett, he was beaten almost daily for over six months, and was harassed and tortured by his jailers.[76]

Who is prone to suicide within jails and prisons? M. Grover indicated that prison suicides occurred among those prisoners who were on remand or awaiting trial.[77] Grover indicated that other groups particularly prone to suicide were violent prisoners, that is, those prisoners convicted of violent offenses.[78] He concluded that those who were most often imprisoned were not at risk.[79]

Grover also pointed out that those most vulnerable to suicide were first-time prisoners.[80] H. Smalley, Grover's successor who was the prison commissioner in 1902, analyzed those prison suicides which occurred between 1902 and 1911. He found that the most striking differences between suicides in prison and ordinary suicides was in respect of their ages: for instance, the incidence of suicides in prison was much higher in the younger age groups.[81] Those convicted of crimes of impulsive violence or crimes against morality (sexual offenses) were found to be most prone to suicides.[82]

E. Dooley, who has published several articles on inmate suicides like, prison suicide in England and Wales 1972-1987, British Journal of Psychiatry, "Non-Natural Deaths in Prison" and the British Journal of Criminology and has done studies on inmate suicide indicated that the most consistent findings of prison suicides have been that a disproportionately number of suicides occurred among prisoners awaiting trial.[83] He further stated that almost half of all prison suicides were found to have a history of attempts at suicide or self-injury.[84]

Inmates who had a history of substance abuse were prone to suicide. According to Winkler, intoxication has been strongly associated with suicide risk in jails.[85] For example, one study found that 85 percent of suicide attempts occurred while intoxicated.[86] Dooley found that 29 percent of his prison suicides had a history of alcohol abuse and 23 percent had a history of drug abuse.[87]

---

76.   Ibid.
77.   Liebling, 18.
78.   Ibid.
79.   Ibid.
80.   Ibid., 17.
81.   Ibid., 8.
82.   Ibid.
83.   Ibid., 42.
84.   Ibid.
85.   Winkler, 320.
86.   Ibid., 321.

In addition, Dooley found that the frequency of drug abuse in the history of prison suicides has increased. S. Backetts, who has conducted studies and has written articles on inmate suicide such as, "Suicides in Scottish Prisons," British Journal of Psychiatry, 1987; "Suicides and Stress in Prison," 1988, found in his study that almost half of the suicides had alcohol, or drug related problems.[88] Backetts indicated that those prisoners who had a history of sexual abuse, which resulted in self-destructive behavior, were prone to suicide.[89]

Those who are prone to suicide was the white male older than 45 years and the white female between the ages of 35 and 65 who were single, and non-white individuals between the ages of 25 and 34.[90] M.L. Hayes, who has conducted studies and has written articles on inmate suicides such as, "And Darkness Closed In," Criminal Justice and Behavior 19883, "National Study of Jail Suicides," Psychiatric Quarterly 1989, found that the typical suicide in jails was white single males in their early 20s.[91] Likewise, Albanese also found that prison inmates who attempted suicide were more often white, single, and with a longer sentence than other inmates.[92] Also, in the Dade County Jail, B.A. Copeland who has conducted studies and written articles on suicide and hangings in prisons and jails such as, "Fatal Suicide Among Non-Whites," American Journal of Forensics Medicine and Pathology 1989, indicated in Lester's study that the typical suicide victim was young, white, male, and with a psychotic background.[93]

Most importantly, this study is concerned with factors that contribute to prison and jail suicides. Overcrowding, deplorable conditions and isolation are factors that contribute to inmate suicide. Overcrowding refers to (more than two inmates to a cell); deplorable conditions refer to (inhumane and an unsanitary environment inside as well as outside the cell); and isolation refers to (placement of an inmate in a cell alone, without light, air, and no contact with other inmates).

The time in which prison and jail suicides occurred emerged as another theme from the literature. According to Road and Faison, the most crucial time for inmates was the first 24 hours in jail.[94] Statistically, this was the period during

---

87. Liebling, 46.
88. Ibid.
89. Ibid., 132-133.
90. Winkler, 319.
91. Lester, 114.
92. Ibid.
93. Ibid.
94. Winkler, 321.

which a disproportionate number of suicides occurred.[95] For instance, different studies have found that 11 out of 17 suicides occurred in the first 24 hours.[96]

Also, Hayes and Rowen indicated that a remarkable 29 percent of suicides occurred in the first three hours of being incarcerated. These authors indicated that the younger, more impulsive individuals tended to commit suicide within the first hours or days after they have been jailed.[97]

R.M. Grover published the first survey of suicides in prison in 1878, indicated that from his study of 81 suicides, and most occurred during the first week in custody.[98] Hayes found that over half of all jail suicides in the United States during 1979 occurred within the first 24 hours of incarceration.

Robert Good, in his study of suicides throughout the Federal penal system and in the state of Maryland from 1964-1969, found that of the 24 completed suicides during that period, most occurred in the early morning or early evening.[99] Good concluded that the hours of 3:00a.m. to 9:00 a.m. and 7:00p.m. to 12:00 midnight covered most of the suicide cases.

Arnett Gaston, in his study of inmate suicides and attempts in New York City Prison System from 1964 to 1971, found that the hours of 5:00 a.m. to 6:00 a.m. to 10:00 p.m. to 12:00 midnight, and 7:00 p.m. to 5:00 p.m. were the most common suicides for suicidal behavior.[100] Also, Gaston indicated that most suicides and attempts occurred during the evening and early morning hours when inmate activity was minimal and correctional staff was also at a minimum.[101]

Dooley's view on the time in which suicides occurred seemed compatible with the views expressed by Gaston and Grover. Almost half of the suicides in Dooley's study occurred between midnight and 8:00 a.m.[102] A quarter of suicides occurred between midnight and 8:00 a.m. when staff supervision was at its lowest.[103]

In sum, a variety of themes on jail and prison suicides have been examined. It appeared that the themes varied according to each school of thought. First, one school of thought argued that deplorable conditions influenced inmate suicides.

---

95. Ibid.
96. Ibid.
97. Ibid.
98. Liebling, 17.
99. Albanese, 66.
100. Ibid.
101. Ibid.
102. Liebling, 49.
103. Ibid.

Another school of thought argued that overcrowding, racism, and lack of trained staff all contributed to inmate suicides. Hence, many of the views expressed by the authors appeared to be overlapping, divergent, and to some extent, a combination of both.

Finally, what has changed about this concept? There has been rudimentary conceptual changes regarding inmate suicides in the United States. It can be strongly concluded that the only change concerning inmate suicides was the definition. From early writers to present day writers, they have been unable to reach a consensus on the definitions of suicide.

Most of all, in light of the literature that has been reviewed, there was one weakness within it. The literature failed to illustrate how isolation contributed to prison and jail suicides. However, the literature clearly exhibited how overcrowding, deplorable conditions, racism, and inadequate staff contributed to prison and jail suicides.

2

METHODOLOGY

H^1: overcrowding contributes to prison and jail inmate suicides.

H^2: deplorable conditions contribute to prison and jail inmate suicides.

H^3: isolation contributes to prison and jail inmate suicides.

Pi: the probability that prisoner i will attempt suicide.

OCi: the degree of overcrowding experienced by prisoner i.

DCi: a measures of the exposure of prisoner i to deplorable conditions.

ISi: the isolation of prisoner i.

Zi: a vector measuring other factors believed to influence the probability of inmates attempting suicide (such as alcohol abuse, drug abuse, previous arrest, length of confinement, those awaiting trial, family perception, self-esteem and offense charged with).

With the above definition, the theory can be reflected in the following model:

$Pi = F(OC_i, DC_i, IS_i; Z_i)$. Where: $\dfrac{d(pi)}{d(OC_i)}, \quad \dfrac{d(i)}{d(DC_i)}, \quad \& \quad \dfrac{d(i)}{d(IS_i)} > 0$

This model simply states the theory symbolically. The equation indicates that the probability of a prisoner attempting suicide is determined by the prisoner's exposure to bad prison conditions as measured by: Overcrowding (OC_i), deplorable conditions (DC_i), and isolation (IS_i), and a set of other control factors represented by Z_i.

The estimating equation for the discrimination analysis could be as follows:

$pi = B_0 + B_1 OC_i + B_2 DC_i + B_3 IS_i + E_i B_i Z_i + U_i.$

B_0 = Intercept term.

B_i = Discriminate coefficient for var i.

In this study, discriminate analysis was employed in the research on jail inmates. Discriminate analysis is a linear combination of the independent variable, which are formed to serve as the basis for assigning cases to groups. There are certain characteristics that must be explained concerning discriminate analysis. First, Wilk's Lambda is sometimes called the U-statistic. When variables are considered individually, Lambda is the ratio of the within-group sum of squares to the total sum of squares. A Lambda of one (1) occurs when all observed group means are equal. Values close to one(1) occur when within-groups variability is small compared to the total variability. A pooled within-group correlation matrix is obtained by averaging the separate co-variance matrices for all groups and the computing of correlation matrix. A total correlation matrix is obtained when all cases are treated as if they are from a single sample.

In this study, I propose to successfully research prison and jail suicides in the state of Mississippi.

I. Problem Statement

The present research seeks to answer the following questions: (1) Does overcrowding in jails cause an inmate to commit suicide? (2) Do deplorable conditions within jail cells cause an inmate to commit suicide? And (3) Does isolation cause inmates to commit suicide?

A survey served as the <u>Instrument</u> consisting of 32 structured questions from the literature (see Index supra p.). The nature of the survey attempted to answer the proposed hypotheses based on the responses given by the inmates.

II. Procedure for Collecting Data

The procedure for collecting data was random sampling. There were 50 detainees chosen voluntarily. The <u>population</u> was to include Alcorn County Jail, Forrest County Jail, Jones County Jail, Lauderdale County Jail, Simpson County Jail, and Hinds County Jail. These five county jails are cited by the United States Justice Department as the worse facilities that housed inmates, after conducting an inspection of all jails in the state of Mississippi.

In this study, 143 inmates were voluntarily selected from Forrest, Jones, and Hinds County Jails. Every inmate was given a chance to participate in the survey interviews at each of these jails. Either these inmates were pre-trial detainees (those awaiting trial), or convicted inmates (those who already had been tried and sentenced). The sample required a number of 50 from the three jail populations, but only Forrest County Jail met this sample number. At the time of the interviews, Forrest County Jail housed over 200 inmates and only those inmates who wanted to participate in the interviews were selected. There were more male than female inmates housed in Forrest County Jail that resulted with more males in this sample.

The same selection process was used at Hinds County Jail. Each inmate was given a chance to participate in the survey in which 47 out of 300 inmates participated. These inmates were housed on four floors of this jail where they were selected.

Also, at the time of the interviews, Jones County Jail housed less than 100 inmates. Again, every inmate was given a chance to participate in the interview. Only 46 wanted to be surveyed and most of these inmates were male: there was a cross-section of pre-trial detainees and convicted inmates who were surveyed.

III. Procedure for Analyzing Data

Sir Ronald Fisher first introduced Discriminat analysis. This technique is used to investigate variables that are important for distinguishing among the groups and to develop a procedure for predicting group membership for new cases whose group membership is undetermined.

Also, in many situations, discriminate analysis, like multiple regression analysis, is used as an exploratory tool. Discriminate analysis begins with the desire to statistically distinguish between two or more groups of cases. These groups are defined by the particular research situation; to distinguish between the groups, the researcher selects a collection of discriminating variables that measure characteristics on which the groups are expected to differ (Source: Norussis, J. Marija. SPSS/PC Advanced Statistics 4.0. Chicago, Illinois: SPSS, Inc., 1990).

In addition, the objective of discriminate analysis is to weight and linearly combine the discriminating variables in some fashion so that the groups are forced to be as statistically distinct as possible. In other words, we want to be able to "discriminate" between the groups in the sense of being able to tell them apart. Once the discriminate functions have been derived, we are able to pursue the two research objectives of this technique: Analysis and classification.

The analysis aspects of this technique provide several tools for the interpretation of data. Among these are statistical tests for measuring the success with the discriminating variables when combined into the discriminate functions. Secondly, the use of discriminate analysis as a classification technique comes after the initial computation. Once a set of variables is found which provides satisfactory discrimination for cases with known group memberships, a set of classification functions can be derived which will permit the classification of new cases with unknown memberships (Sources: Nie, H. Norman, et al. <u>SPSS Statistical Package for the Social Sciences</u>. New York: McGraw-Hill Book Company, 1975).

IV. <u>Dependent Variable</u>

The dependent variable is classified as those inmates who attempted suicide (variable 21) because it best represents the population under study. By identifying these inmates who tried to take their life after being incarcerated, indicates that this particular group is more likely to commit suicide than those inmates who have not experienced any history of attempted suicides.

Cross-tabulation was employed for this isolated group who had attempted suicide in order to determine how they responded based on race, gender, educational level, history of substance abuse (alcohol, drugs), previous arrests, length of confinement, and those awaiting trial (independent variables). These independent or predictor variables were cross-tabbed with the dependent variable, attempted suicide. Out of 143 inmates surveyed, 11 had attempted suicide (4 females, 7 males; 7 African-Americans, 2 Whites, 2 Hispanics).

Their ages ranged from 18 years old to 32 years of age that attempted suicide. Five had less than a high school education, three had graduated from high school and three had attended college but did not graduate.

These 11 respondents were asked, "had there ever been a history of substance abuse" and two had a history of alcohol abuse while eight had not experienced alcohol abuse. Only four had experienced drug abuse and six had not with seven having experienced previous arrest, while four had not experienced previous arrest. I also asked these inmates "how long had they been confined" and 7 of 11 had been confined less than six months.

LIMITATIONS

In the present research, certain restrictions should be noted. First, the population in the research focused on only those jails in the state of Mississippi. These inmates served as the sample that were not a representative of the general population of prisoners. Therefore, I cannot generalize about the entire population of inmates.

EDUCATIONAL SIGNIFICANCE

In this research, we wanted to conduct research on inmate suicides because of the recent incidents which occurred in Mississippi jails. We hope that this research will be successful in raising the public's attention to the problems within Mississippi jails that have led inmates to commit suicide. By raising public awareness of the jail conditions in the state of Mississippi, perhaps, we as a society can derive at some meaningful solutions.

Further, I proposed to interview 50 inmates from six jails in Mississippi. However, I was only allowed to conduct interviews in three of these jails, these being Forrest County Jail, Jones County Jail, and Hinds County Jail. Hinds County Jail was chosen because of its location, not because of any violations by the Justice Department's recent investigation on Mississippi jails. Due to the transference of inmates from Alcorn County Jail to the state penitentiary, interviews were not conducted. Due to the fear held by Sheriff Hill, I was not allowed interviews at Lauderdale County Jail.

3

JAIL DESCRIPTION AND DEMOGRAPHICS

I. Forrest:

A. Population-68,314

B. Racial Make-up-(White: 47,050; Non-White: 21,820)

C. Average Income-$19,119

(Source: <u>Mississippi Statistical Abstract: Division on Research</u>, 1993)

    Forrest County jail is located in Hattiesburg, Mississippi, which was the first jail visited. Forrest County Jail is a large facility with adequate staff and personnel. After arriving at this jail, I was escorted to the second floor where the interviews were conducted. The visiting police officer (person who oversees or is in charge of visitation procedurals) explained a few procedures before the inmates were brought out of their cells. The area in which I sat up my interviews was the same area where the inmates receive visits. This area was very clean, neat, and with a pine soil scent that had a pleasant smell.

    There was a black steel cage with minute holes in it mounted down in the floor in the same area where the interviews were given. The visiting officer explained that this cage was called a "bull pen" which segregates the inmates from their visitors. This bullpen is designed to prohibit transference of any items from the visitors to the inmate during visitations. Also, there was a camera assembled in the upper corner of the ceiling on this same floor where the inmates were interviewed. The camera monitored the behavior of inmates during visitations and insured that no unusual objects were passed through the bullpen.

As the male inmates were released from their cells, they walked out in the interview room in a single file line moving like military soldiers. These inmates were extremely quiet as they answered the surveys. They had no smiles on their faces but appeared to be relieved by being out of their cells. I also noticed that the inmate wore house shoes or tennis shoes without shoe-strings. After the male inmates were surveyed, they returned tot heir cells and the female inmates were escorted to the second floor. The female inmates were a lot more loquacious than the male inmates were. They complained about how their meals were not enough to satisfy their insatiable appetites. These female inmates complained about it being overcrowded on the women ward that slept on the floor. Before the interviews were over, the female inmates indicated that "being in jail was like being in purgatory". They also emphasized that there was no exercise room for them, nothing but "concrete ground"

(September 1, 1994 interviews conducted: Officer Tom Phillips, Visitation Officer).

II. Jones County:

A. Population-62,031

B. Racial Make-up-(White: 46,090; Non-White: 15,800)

C. Average Income-$18,754

(Source: Mississippi Statistical Abstract: Division on Research, 1993)

Jones County Jail is located in Laurel Mississippi where the second interviews were conducted. After I arrive at this jail, I was devastated at the sight of this jail. This facility was not only horrible from the outside, but the inside as well. The building itself looked as if it would collapse at any time where cracks eroded the 18th Century structure. The jail was very small in size as well as small in adequate personnel. The officer led the way to the second floor where the inmates were housed and where the interviews took place. This area was equipped with exercise furniture and old law books. The second floor was very dirty, had a foul odor, leaking roof, unclean jail cells, overcrowded cells, and lack of an air conditioner.

Even more, at the time of the interviews there were officers who indicated that a new facility was underway. Chief Nelson indicated that Jones County

Jail had the space to house only 72 inmates in such a restricted facility. Chief Nelson also stated that at least one (1) suicide had occurred in this jail. The victim was a 38-year-old white female who allegedly committed suicide on August 20, 1991 in where the suicide occurred in less than 24 hours of incarceration. Chief Nelson revealed that the female victim had a history of substance abuse, family problems and was awaiting trial.

Both male and female inmates were led out of their cells into the exercise area where the interviews took place. Some of the inmates were very conversant and others were not. Those who were very loquacious asked questions about their research. These inquisitive inmates wanted to know whether this research would help their situation. Also, these inmates appeared to be more knowledgeable about the alleged suicides across the state of Mississippi. They also were more eager to learn more about their research topic and were most friendly and at times, humorous.

During the course of the interviews, there was one inmate who was locked down or isolated from other inmates. It was extremely dark in his cell and there was not much room to move around inside of it. However, this inmate managed to extend his hand from an open hole to shake my assistant's hand as well as my hand before we departed from the jail (September 8, 1994 interviews conducted).

III. <u>Hinds County</u>:

A. Population-254,441

B. Racial Make-up-(White: 123,800; Non-White: 131,930)

C. Average Income-$22,199

(Source: Mississippi Statistical Abstract: Division on Research)

Hinds County Jail is located in Jackson, Mississippi where the questionnaires were distributed to the inmates because interviews were not permitted due to the transference of inmates to the new jail facility in Raymond, Mississippi.

Attorney Homer Best is the jailhouse lawyer for the inmates in Hinds County Jail. He was in charge of the distribution of surveys in which instructions were given on how the surveys were to be administered. However, I did get a chance to visit the Hinds County Jail and observed the conditions in this facility (October 8, 1993 visitation allowed). I was allowed to tour each floor that the rabbles were housed. From the first floor tot he fourth floor of the jail, it was very neat, clean and with a pleasant scent. Even though this was a large facility, it experienced over-crowding. The number of inmates exceeded the number of beds and there were more than two inmates to a cell. This problem existed on every floor I toured.

In addition, I was allowed to sit in an empty cell similar to where the inmates were housed. Within this cell there were no windows, no wash sink, no decent bed to sleep on. The object I sat on was nothing but a hard, uncomfortable piece of slab that these inmates had to sleep on. It was a lonely and a cold feeling sitting in this cell that was no bigger than a match-box.

Furthermore, at least three alleged suicides have occurred in this jail since 1987. In 1989, on April 7, Tony Brakefield, a 21-year-old black male alleg-edly committed suicide but no background information was available on this victim. In 1992, on June 27, Norman Hendrix, a 44-year-old black male allegedly committed suicide and background information was unobtainable on this victim. In 1993, on February 20, Bobby Everett, a 19-year-old black male allegedly committed suicide, and no background information were available on this victim (Source: Mississippi State Medical Examiner's Office).

IV. Hangings in Mississippi Jails, Prisons: 1987-1993

This chart shows the number of deaths that have occurred in Mississippi jails since 1987 plus two recent deaths that are not illustrated in this chart. This chart was taken from the Jackson Advocate Newspaper Archives, (1993, Jackson, Mississippi). Of Mississippi's 47 jail and prison hangings reported by the State Medical Examiner's office since 1987 and ruled suicides (alleg-edly), nearly a third of those who died were 25 or younger. Four were juve-niles-two 14 and two 16.

1987 TOTAL: 6

DATE	COUNTY	NAME	AGE	RACE/SEX
5/29	Lee	Ricky Russell	34	WM

6/19	Harrison	Edward McLemore	30	BM
7/13	Chickasaw	Son Hoobson	N/A	BM
11/9	Lee	James Kelly	48	WM
12/5	Jackson	Robert MacMillan	29	BM
12/20	Itawamba	Ricky Gilliland	25	WM

1988 TOTAL: 7

3/4	Winston	Willie Cooper	35	WM
5/1	Lafayette	L.V. Jones	47	BM
6/3	Union	Craig Keys	19	BM
8/28	Harrison	Charles Kiester	N/A	WM
10/15	*Sunflower	Gregory Jefferson	26	BM
12/12	Harrison	Everett Uplinger	58	WM
12/28	Lowndes	Genie Irvin	N/A	WM

1989 TOTAL: 14

1/5	Tunica	Ronald Bogan	16	BM
2/21	Quitman	Berbard Roberson	21	WM
3/17	Simpson	Willie Smith	29	BM
3/23	Alcorn	Joel Simmons	34	WM
4/7	Hinds	Tony Brakefield	21	BM
4/10	Pontotoc	David McGowan	49	WM
4/14	Warren	Melvinn Ellis	14	WM
5/4	Tallahatchie	Willie Qualls	31	BM
5/23	Monroe	Bounmy Douangprasent	38	WM
5/24	Washington	Tijuana Barney	14	BF
6/17	Lee	Leslie Smith	26	BM
7/4	Alcorn	Tina Hare	23	WF

9/3	Lauderdale	Anthony Whitehead	28	WM
10/19	Lincoln	Glenda Durr	30	WF

1990 TOTAL: 5

4/15	Grenda	Ed Dunn	25	BM
7/6	Sunflower	Eugene Ware	35	BM
7/26	Oktibbeha	Ronald Franklin	30	WM
10/10	Neshoba	David Scott Campbell	21	BM
11/16	Itawamba	David Hood	21	WM

1991 TOTAL: 5

5/4	Scott	Alexander Barton	26	WM
6/29	Benton	Lonnie Cole	50	BM
8/15	Bolivar	Carl Walker	35	BM
8/20	Jones	Shirley Powelson	38	WF
8/24	Harrison	Donald Page	33	WM

1992 TOTAL: 8

5/21	Sunflower	Shannon King	18	BM
5/24	Scott	Sherry Ratliff	24	BF
6/27	Hinds	Norman Hendrix	44	BM
8/22	Simpson	Andrea Jones	18	BM
9/30	Rankin	Mary Sorrell	32	BF
10/9	Copiah	Kenneth Royce Sills	42	WM
10/14	Pontotoc	Ricky Lee Galloway	16	WM
11/6	Stone	Peter Shannon	23	BM

1993 TO DATE: 2

2/20	Hinds	Bobby Everett	19	BM
2/21	Adams	Chris Wayne Rodriguez	18	WM

*Hanging at state prison

II. Data Analysis

I. Characteristics of the Sample

In this study, I hypothesized that overcrowding (more than two inmates in a cell, or when the number of inmates exceed the number of beds), deplorable conditions refer to (inhumane and an unsanitary environment inside the cell such as being forced to consume meals close to filthy, smelly toilets), and isolation refers to (placement of inmates in a dark, cold, and lonely cell without contact with other inmates) contributes to inmate suicide.

In this research, I surveyed 143 inmates. Out of 143 inmates, there were 26 females and 117 males. From Forrest County Jail, there were 7 females and 43 males; from Jones County Jail, there were 4 females and 43 males; and from Hinds County Jail, there were 15 females and 31 males (See Table-1-1).

Table 1-1. Percentage of Male and Female Inmates in Forrest, Jones and Hinds County Jails, 1994.

GENDER	FORREST	JONES	HINDS	TOTAL
Female	4.9%(7)	2.8%(4)	10.5%(15)	18.2%(26)
Male	30.1%(43)	30.1%(43)	21.7%(31)	81.8%(117)

There were 107 African-Americans, 33 Anglo-Saxons, and 2 Hispanics. From Forrest County Jail, there were 37 African-Americans, 11 Anglo-Saxons, and 2 Hispanics; from Jones County Jail, there were 38 African-Americans, and 8 Anglo-Saxons; and from Hinds County Jail, 32 African-Americans and 14 Anglo-Saxons (See Table 1-2 on next page).

Table 1-2. Percentage of Race of Inmates in Forrest, Jones and Hinds County Jails, 1994.

RACE	FORREST	JONES	HINDS	TOTAL
African-American	26.1%(37)	26.8%(38)	22.5%(32)	75.4%(107)
Anglo-Saxons	7.7%(11)	5.6%(8)	9.9%(14)	23.2%(33)
Hispanic	1.4%(2)	---------	---------	1.4%(2)

Their current ages ranged from 15-years-old to 73-years-old. From Forrest County Jail, 17 years was the youngest and 47 was the oldest; from

Jones County Jail, 15 was the youngest and 51 was the oldest; and from Hinds County Jail, 17 was the youngest and 73 the oldest.

Also, out of 143 inmates, 24 were currently married, 20 were divorced, 8 were separated, 8 were living together unmarried, 77 were single, and 5 indicated other. From Forrest County Jail, 11 were currently married, 6 were currently divorced, 5 were currently separated, 2 were living together unmarried, 23 were currently single, and 2 indicated other.

Table 1-3. Percentage of Present Marital Status of Inmates from Forrest, Jones, and Hinds County Jails, 1994.

MARITAL ST.	FORREST	JONES	HINDS	TOTAL
Married	7.7%(11)	5.6%(8)	3.5%(5)	16.9%(24)
Divorced	4.2%(6)	2.8%(4)	7.0%(10)	14.1%(20)
Separated	3.5%(5)	2.1%(3)	2.1%(3)	5.6%(8)
Unmarried	1.4%(2)	2.1%(3)	2.1%(3)	5.6%(8)
Single	16.2%(23)	20.4%(29)	17.6%(25)	54.2%(77)
Other	1.4%(2)	----------	2.1%(3)	3.2%(55)

From Jones County Jail, 8 were currently married, 4 were currently divorced, 3 were currently separated, 3 were currently living together unmarried, and 29 were single. From Hinds County Jail, 5 were currently married, 10 were currently divorced, 3 were living together unmarried, 25 were single and 3 indicated other.

Further, the education level of the inmates differed from each population. For example, there were 48 inmates who had less than high school (those who didn't received a diploma); 55 had finished high school, 23 of the inmates had less than a college education (those who didn't receive degrees); 73 had received a college degree, and 4 had gone beyond a 4-year degree.

Table 1-4. Percentage of Educational Level of Inmates from Forrest, Jones, and Hinds County Jails, 1994.

EDUCATION LEVEL	FORREST	JONES	HINDS	TOTAL
Less Than High School	8.4%(12)	15.4%(22)	9.8%(14)	33.6%(48)
High School Graduate	13.3%(19)	12.6%(18)	12.6%(18)	38.5%(55)
Less Than College	7.0%(10)	3.5%(5)	5.6%(8)	16.1%(23)
College Graduate	4.2%(6)	1.4%(2)	3.5%(5)	9.1%(13)
Beyond 4-Yr College	2.1%(3)	----------	.7%(1)	2.8%(4)

From Forrest County Jail, there was a higher literacy rate in terms of education obtained. There were 6 who graduated from college, 3 had gone beyond a 4-year degree, 19 had graduated from high school, 10 who attended college but did not graduate, and 12 had less than high school (See table 1-4 above).

However, Jones County Jail had the highest illiteracy rate in terms of education obtained and reading level. Out of 46 who were interviewed, more than 10 could not read or barely write. There were 22 who received less than a high school education, 18 had graduated from high school, 5 attended college but didn't graduate, and 2 were college graduates.

From Hinds County Jail, 74 received less than a high school education, 188 were high school graduates, 8 attended college but did not graduate, 5 were college graduates, and 1 had gone beyond a 4 year college degree.

Out of the 143 inmates surveyed, I asked, "had there been previous arrests," and 98 had previous arrests while 43 had not experienced any previous arrests.

Table 1-5. Percentage of Previous Arrests of Inmates from Forrest, Jones, and Hinds County Jails, 1994.

ARREST	FORREST	JONES	HINDS	TOTAL
Previous	22.7%(32)	24.1%(34)	22.7%(32)	69.5%(98)
No Prev.	12.1%(17)	8.5%(12)	9.9%(14)	30.5%(43)

From Forrest County Jail, 32 had previous arrests, 17 had no previous arrest; from Jones County Jail, 34 had previous arrests and 12 had none; while 32 had previous arrests from Hinds County Jail only, 14 had none.

In addition, I asked the inmates how many times they had been arrested. Fifty-six had been arrested 1 to 3 times; 15 had been arrested 4 to 6 times, 3 had been arrested 7 to 9 times, and 13 had 10 or more arrests (career criminals).

Table 1-6. Percentage Number of Arrest of Inmates from Forrest, Jones, and Hinds County Jails, 1994.

NUMBER OF ARRESTS	FORREST	JONES	HINDS	TOTAL
1-3 Times	24.1%(21)	20.7%(18)	19.5%(17)	64.4%(56)
4-6 Times	6.9%(6)	5.7%(5)	4.6%(4)	17.2%(15)
7-9 Times	1.1%(1)	2.3%(2)	---------	3.4%(3)
10 or More	1.1%(1)	9.2%(8)	44.6%(4)	14.9%(13)

From Forrest County Jail, 21 had from 1 to 3 arrests, 6 had been arrested 4 to 6 times, 1 had 7 to 9 arrests, and 1 had been arrested 10 or more times. From Jones County Jail, 18 had 1 to 3 arrests, 5 had from 4 to 6 arrests, 2 had 7 to 9 arrests, and 8 had 10 or more arrests; from Hinds County Jail, 17 had been arrested 1 to 3 times, 4 had been arrested 4 to 6 times, and 4 had been arrested 10 or more times.

II. SUBSTANTIVE CONTENT

In my hypothesis, I hypothesized that overcrowding was one of three factors which contributed to inmate suicide. According to John Wooldredge and Thomas Winfree, the higher degree of overcrowding corresponded with greater numbers of inmate suicide and natural deaths. Out of 143 inmates that were surveyed, 14 indicated that overcrowding was a reason why inmates commit suicide.

From the Forrest County Jail, 8 stated that overcrowding was reason inmates commit suicide, and 1 from Hinds County Jail indicated that overcrowding was a reason why inmates commit suicide.

Alison Liebling indicated that overcrowding in prisons was often linked in some way to suicide. For example, rates of illness complaints, levels of psychological stress and death rates have been found to be disproportionately high in overcrowded prisons. There were 20 inmates who indicated that depression caused by overcrowding was a reason why inmates commit suicide.

Further, deplorable conditions are another factor that contributes to jail inmate suicide. According to Hickerson-Smith, inmate who had been forced to consume meals in close proximity to toilets provoked feelings of anger and disgust. Out of 143 inmates, 15 indicated that deplorable conditions contributed to inmate suicide. Inmates from Forrest County Jail (4) indicated that deplorable conditions contributed to inmate suicide; 7 inmates from Jones County Jail indicated that deplorable conditions contributes to inmate suicides; and 4 inmates from Hinds County Jail indicated likewise (See Table 1-7 below).

Table 1-7. Percentage of Factors Contributing to Inmate Suicide From Forrest, Jones, and Hinds County Jails, 1994.

FACTORS	FORREST	JONES	HINDS	TOTAL
Over-crowding	6.7%(8)	4.2%(5)	.8%(1)	11.7%(14)
Deplorable	3.3%(4)	5.8%(7)	3.3%(4)	12.5%(15)
Isolation	2.5%(3)	5.0%(6)	3.3%(4)	10.8%(13)
Lack of Trained Staff	1.7%(2)	.8%(1)	.8%(1)	3.3%(4)
Lack of Adequate Facilities	--------	--------	2.5%(3)	2.5%(3)
All the Above	14.2%(17)	8.3%(10)	8.3%(10)	30.8%(37)

Also, Hickerson-Smith indicated that cramped cell conditions and lack of outdoor recreation lowered self-esteem. Out of 143 surveyed, 52 were very satisfied with themselves, 36 were somewhat satisfied, 26 were not satisfied with self, 26 were very unsatisfied with themselves (see table 1-8).

Table 1-8. Self-Esteem of Inmates from Forrest, Jones and Hinds County Jails, 1994.

SELF-ESTEEM	FORREST	JONES	HINDS	TOTAL
Very Satisfied	5.7%(8)	15.0%(21)	16.4%(23)	37.1%(52)
Somewhat Satisfied	9.3%(13)	5.7%(8)	10.7%(15)	25.7%(36)
Not Satisfied	10.7%(15)	4.3%(6)	3.6%(5)	18.6%(26)
Very Unsatisfied	9.3%(13)	7.1%(10)	2.1%(3)	18.6%(26)

From Forrest County Jail, 8 were very satisfied with themselves, 13 were somewhat satisfied with themselves, 15 were not satisfied with themselves, and 13 were very unsatisfied with themselves.

From Jones County Jail, 21 were very satisfied with self, 8 were somewhat satisfied, 6 were not satisfied, and 10 were very unsatisfied with themselves; from Hinds County Jail, 23 were very satisfied with themselves, 15 were somewhat satisfied, 5 were not satisfied, and 3 were very unsatisfied with themselves.

Meanwhile, I asked the inmates did they receive visits from family and if so, how often were the visits. Out of the 143 surveyed, 32 received visits from family less than once a week, 49 received visits from family 1 to 2 times per week, 16 received family visits once a month, 24 received family visits 3 to 4 times a month.

Table 1-9. Family Visits to Inmates From Forrest, Jones, and Hinds County Jails, 1994.

VISITS	FORREST	JONES	HINDS	TOTAL
Less Than Once A Week	6.6%(8)	13.2%(16)	6.6%(8)	26.4%(32)
1-2 Times Per Week	9.1%(11)	15.7%(19)	15.7%(19)	40.5%(49)
Once Per Month	4.1%(5)	5.0%(6)	4.1%(5)	13.2%(16)
3-4 Times Per Month	13.2%(16)	.8%(1)	5.8%(7)	19.8%(24)

From Forrest County Jail, 8 received less than once a week family visits, 11 received 1 to 2 times per week family visits; 5 received family visits once a month and 16 received family visits 3 to 4 times a month.

From Jones County Jail, 16 received family visits less than once a week, 19 received family visits 1 to 2 times per week, and 6 received family visits once a month; and 1 inmate received family visits 3 to 4 times a month.

From Hinds County Jail, 8 received family visits less than once a week, 19 received family visits 1 to 2 times per week, 5 received family visits once a month, and 7 received family visits 3 to 4 times a month. There were 22 of the inmates out of 143 who received no family visits.

Isolation was the third factor that contributes to inmate suicide. According to Gregory Winkler, isolation increases the risk of suicide among inmates. Earl Grollman indicated that it was isolation within the cell that contributes to the high occurrence of suicide as a result of lock-down(see Table 1-7.).

Out of 143 inmates that were surveyed, 13 stated that isolation was indeed a cause of inmate suicide. From Forrest County Jail, 3 indicated that isolation contributes to suicide, 6 from Jones County Jail indicated that isolation contributes to suicide and 4 from Hinds County stated that isolation contributes to suicide (see Table 1-7.).

Even though lack of trained staff and lack of adequate facilities were not included as factors influencing inmate suicides, some inmates thought that these factors influenced inmate suicides. There were 4 who indicated that a lack of trained staff, and 3 indicated that lack of adequate facilities contributes to inmate suicide.

Most importantly, out of 143 inmates surveyed, 37 indicated that all these factors contribute to inmate suicide. For instance 17 inmates from Forrest County Jail indicated all the above; 10 from Jones County Jail also indicated all the above, and 10 from Hinds County Jail indicated all the above (see Table 1-7.).

Also, according to M. Grover, those who are awaiting trial or on remand were prone to suicide. Out of 143 inmates interviewed, 68 were awaiting trial and 61 had been convicted. From Forrest County Jail, 21 were awaiting trail, 21 from Jones County Jail and 26 from Hinds County Jail were awaiting trial.

Table 1-10. Percentage of Inmates Awaiting Trial and Convicted From Forrest, Jones and Hinds County Jail, 1994.

	FORREST	JONES	HINDS	TOTAL
YES	15.6%(21)	15.0%(21)	18.6%(26)	48.6%(68)
NO	15.7%(22)	15.0%(21)	12.9%(18)	43.6%(61)
OTHER	4.3%(6)	2.1%(3)	1.4%(2)	7.9%(11)

However, 22 from Forest County Jail had been convicted, 21 from Jones County Jail had been convicted, and 18 from Hinds County Jail had been convicted while 6 from Forrest County Jail, 3 from Jones County Jail, and 2 from Hinds County Jail indicated other.

III. <u>GROUP CLASSIFICATION</u>

By group classification, we mean that the independent variable was placed into one group and those variables (dependent) were placed in another group. In this sample, the major independent variables that were grouped was overcrowding, deplorable conditions, and isolation. There were several predictor variables such as drug abuse, alcohol abuse, those awaiting trial, offense committed, family's perception of inmate, self-esteem of inmates, and attempted suicide were grouped. The dependent variable is classified as those inmates who attempted suicide.

In this aspect, I ask the question, is there any relationship between the history of substance abuse and attempted suicide? Is there any relationship between those awaiting trial and attempted suicide? Is there any relationship between the offense committed and attempted suicide? Is there any relationship between family's perception of inmate and attempted suicide? And, is there any relationship between self-esteem of inmates and attempted suicide?

By grouping the major and minor variables together, we can predict whether or not there is a correlation between these variables and inmate suicide. We will refer tot he Canonical Correlation, Wilks' Lambda, Chi-square, Degree of freedom and the Significance level to show the statistics of those variables that affect the dependent variable the most.

IV. <u>FINDINGS</u>

The canonical correlation for the independent variable isolation was 0.09; meaning that there is a positive and moderate correlation between those inmates who have been isolated, and factors influencing inmate suicide (overcrowding, deplorable conditions, isolation). Wilks' Lambda showed a 0.9 which means that there is a high degree of association between isolation of inmates, factors influencing inmate suicide, and attempted suicide. The Chi-Square is .134, degree of freedom is 3 and the level of significance is 0.71.

What is the nature of relationship of those inmates being isolated and attempted suicide? Attempted suicide variable showed a 0.6, factors influencing inmate suicide showed a 0.50. These statistics indicate that as attempts of suicide increase where there is overcrowding and deplorable conditions, isolation decreases. Only 36 of 143 inmates had experienced isolation, and 11 of 143 attempted suicide.

There is a positive and moderate relationship between self-esteem and attempted suicide. The canonical correlation is 0.19 for this variable, Wilks' Lambda is 0.95 meaning that there is a higher degree of association between self-esteem and attempted suicide. The level of significance showed a 0.76 resulting as a small chance that an inmates self-esteem is more likely to influence attempts of suicide where there is an occurrence of overcrowding, deplorable conditions and isolation. Out of 143 surveyed, 26 inmates were very unsatisfied with themselves.

There is a positive and moderate relationship between the family's perception of the inmate and attempted suicide. The canonical correlation was 0.23, while Wilks' Lambda showed a 0.93 indicating that there is a high degree of association between family's perception and attempted suicide. Chi-Square is 99.4, degree of freedom was 9, and the significance level was 0.39. The function for attempted suicide showed a -0.57 and the function for factors influencing suicide showed a 0.93. These statistics indicate that as the family's perception or level of concern for the inmate increases, attempts at suicide decrease. There were 101 inmates who indicated that their family cared a great deal.

There is a positive and moderate relationship between those inmates who are awaiting trial and attempted suicide. Canonical correlation showed a 0.21, and Wilks' Lambda showed a 0.95, meaning that there is a high degree of association between those awaiting trial and attempted suicide. The significant level showed a 0.10 indicating that these correlations are statistical significant.

There is a positive and moderate correlation between history of alcohol abuse and attempted suicide. The canonical correlation showed a 0.04, Wilks' Lambda showed a 0.99; meaning that there is a high degree of association between alcohol abuse and attempted suicide. However, the level of significance showed a 0.96 indicating that this is statistically insignificant. For example, the function for attempted suicide showed a 0.45 indicating that as alcohol abuse decreases, attempted suicide increases. Only 35 inmates had a history of alcohol abuse.

There is a moderate and positive correlation between history of drug abuse and attempted suicide. The canonical correlation showed a 0.12, while Wilks' Lambda showed a 0.98 and the significant level showed a 0.54. Lambda indicates that there is a high degree of association between history of drug abuse and attempted suicides. The significant level indicate that these correlations are statistical significant. There were 45 inmates who had a history of drug abuse.

Even more, there is a moderate correlation between offense charged with and attempted suicide. The canonical correlation showed a 0.2, Lambda showed a 0.99, and the significant level showed a 0.54. Lambda indicates that there is a high degree of association between offense charged with and attempted suicide. The significance level indicates that these correlations are statistically significant. There were 36 who had drug offense charges, 19 had been charged with robbery, 11 were charged with murder, and 3 were charged with sexual assault, while 64 indicated other (DUI, shoplifting, aggravated assault, violation of probation) and 9 were charged with auto theft.

In order to analyze these 11 inmates who attempted suicide, separating this group from the other group of inmates (132) in this study, discriminate analysis was again employed to determine whether the separating group answered any differently to the independent or predictor variables than the other group. Based on the data output, the discriminate score showed that there is a moderate correlation between the dependent variable (the 11 who attempted suicide) and alcohol abuse. The canonical correlation showed a 0.557 and the canonical discriminate function coefficient for variable 09 was 0.500 (see Figure 2.1b).

Figure 2.1: Canonical Discriminate Functions

Function	Eigenvalue	Percent of Variance	Cumulative Percent	Canonical Correlation
*1	0.500	100.00	100.00	0.577

*Marks the 1 canonical discriminate functions remaining

It is important to emphasize that the canonical correlation measures the degree of association between the discriminate scores and the grouped variables.

Figure 2.1b: Standardized Canonical Discriminate Function Coefficients

Variables (Predictor)	Function 1
VAR 09 (Alcohol Abuse)	0.50000
VAR 10(Drug Abuse)	1.00000
VAR 11 (Previous Arrest)	1.06066
VAR 31 (Offense Charged With)	1.41421

Figure 2.1b indicates that variable 09 has the highest correlation with the discriminate function which has the most discriminating power than variable 10, 1, and 31 which was the lowest correlation with the discriminate function or (dependent variable; attempted suicide).

Figure 2.2: Pooled Within-Groups Correlation Between Discriminating Variables and Canonical Discriminate Functions

Variables (Predictor)	Function 1
VAR 33(Self-Esteem)	0.78446
VAR 11 (Previous Arrests)	-0.70711
VAR 23 (If you thought about it)	0.55902
VAR 10 (Drug Abuse)	0.50000
VAR 32 (Awaiting Trial)	0.35355
VAR 31 (Offense Charged With)	-0.17678
VAR 13 (Length of Confinement)	-0.17678
VAR 09 (Alcohol Abuse)	0.00000

By looking at the groups of variables which have coefficients of different signs, we can determine which variable values result in large and small function values. In this Figure, variable 33 has the highest correlation with the discriminate function. Variable 11 has the second largest correlation in absolute value. The negative signs indicate that small function values are associated with the presence of attempted suicide; however, these large coefficients contribute most to the overall discriminate function. Also, if you compare Figure 2.1b and Figure 2.2 you will notice that more variables are analyzed in Figure 2.2 because of the differences that exist among this group.

Figure 2.3: Classification Analysis of Control Factors Influencing Inmate Suicide 1994.

CONTROL FACTORS	$\bar{X}$=GROUP I (ATTEMPTED SUICIDE)	$\bar{X}$=GROUP II (NON-ATTEMPT)	N=TOTAL
Alcohol Abuse	1.66	1.66	1.66
Drug Abuse	1.66	1.33	1.50
Previous Arrest	1.33	1.00	1.16
Offense Chgd With	4.66	5.00	4.83
Awaiting Trial	1.33	2.00	1.66
Self-Esteem	2.00	2.66	2.33
Length of Confinement	1.00	1.33	1.16
Family Perception	1.00	1.33	1.16

In the above figure, the mean or average (x) is shown representing the control factors of Group I and II. The last column represents the individual total (N) score of the mean for both groups.

The mean score for alcohol abuse is the same for both groups. The mean for drug abuse for Group I is greater than the mean for Group II. This score indicates that those inmates who attempted suicide had a higher history of drug abuse than the inmates who had not attempted suicide. The mean for previous arrest for Group I is greater than the mean for Group II which indicates that these inmates who attempted suicide had been arrested more times than those inmates represented in Group II.

The mean for offense charged with is less than Group II compared with Group I because this variable was divided into categories that resulted in responses varying. Also, the mean for awaiting trial is less than for those inmates who attempted suicide than the non-attempts indicating that the inmates represented in Group I had been convicted.

The mean for self-esteem in Group I is less than the mean for Group II. Group I mean score implies that the self-esteem for this group is lower among attempters of suicide. The mean score for length of confinement and family perception were less for Group I than for Group II.

4

CONCLUSION

When applying any statistical tool in research, one must analyze the level of significance in order to determine whether to accept or reject a hypothesis. In this study, the statistical tool utilized was discriminate analysis or the U-statistics. In analyzing this data, the three characteristics that make up discriminate were examined; canonical correlation, Wilks' lambda, and the significance level. Attention was given to the canonical correlations and Wilks' Lambda, but the significance level was the characteristic that served as the verdict of accepting or rejecting a research hypothesis. How is this determined? If the significance level ranges from 0.01 to 0.05, then it is considered statistically significant. However, if the significance level exceeds 0.05, then it is considered statistically insignificant.

Based on this data, there were disparities with the level of significance. Some of the major independent variables, when grouped with the dependent variables, showed high significance levels. However, when some of my minor independent variables were grouped with the dependent variable, the level of significance was low.

As an illustration, such variables as self-esteem, substance abuse, family's perception, offense committed, those awaiting trial, showed a low significance level when grouped with the dependent variable as a result being statistically significant. When major variables, such as isolation, overcrowding, and deplorable conditions showed a high significance level when grouped with the same dependent variable as a result being statistically insignificant.

In conclusion, these statistics have shown that there are other factors which influence inmates committing suicide, other than overcrowding, isolation, and deplorable conditions. I fail to reject my research hypothesis. Even though the latter variables showed that there was a high degree of association between attempted suicide and these factors, the level of significance was to high.

In sum, it is also important to make some comments about certain questions on the questionnaire in the Appendix as well as those questions omitted or failed to include in the survey. First, question number 19 is restricted to attempted suicides by prisoners after confinement in jail. Questions 17, 18 and 21 are not mutually exclusive therefore, creating overlapping categories.

The survey did not include specific questions pertaining to the current conditions in the jails which were visited (Forrest, Jones, and Hinds). Such conditions as overcrowding and deplorable were visible during the interviews which were recorded; however, absentee of these specific questions from the survey may have resulted in the rejection of hypothesis 1 and 2 (overcrowding contributes to inmate suicide, H2: Deplorable conditions contribute to inmate suicide).

However, there were specific questions on the survey that addressed hypothesis 3(isolation contributes to inmate suicide) which resulted in a high degree of association between attempted suicide and those inmates being isolated, but was statistically insignificant. Even though these hypotheses showed a positive correlation as well as a high degree of association of the dependent variable (attempted suicide), they were statistically insignificant because their significant levels exceeded 0.5. There were questions on the survey that addressed the causes or reasons why inmates committed suicide. The data indicated that the majority of the inmates surveyed thought that depression or psychological problems along with lack of self-esteem contributed most to inmate suicide.

Finally, by rejecting these hypotheses does not indicate that these physical conditions in jails (over-crowding, deplorable conditions, and isolation) are not associated with jail inmate suicide, but that there are other factors along with these factors that contribute to suicide among jail inmates. Perhaps, this study has opened the doors for counter-arguments-I welcome such critics! Chapter 5 serves as a new addition to this Master's Thesis that was not included in the original study in 1995. Chapter 5 revisits the thesis topic of inmate suicide in Mississippi Jails since 1995.

5

PRISONERS' DEATHS IN LOCAL MISSISSIPPI COUNTY JAILS: AN EMPIRICAL STUDY REVISITED

<u>Introduction</u>

This chapter is an outgrowth of my Master's Thesis conducted in 1995.[1] Therefore, the major objective in this chapter are threefold: first, to analyze change in Mississippi jails since 1995 and secondly, to replicate empirical findings from initial suicide study conducted in 1995.[2] Afterwards, and third, to revisit Durkheim's theory of suicide by testing his theory regarding structural forces that influence suicide. The same inmates surveyed in 1995 are not the same inmates who were surveyed in 1999. The environment of each jail has changed since the original study was conducted. There have been upgrades in two Mississippi county jails. New jails have been built at the Lauderdale County Jail and Jones County Jail as a result of a U.S. Justice Department order issued by former Attorney General Janet Reno. Thus, this is not a longitudinal study, but one of replication only. This chapter is important because it provides a frame of reference in uncovering those fac-

---

1. Lisa Nikol Nealy. *Prisoners' Deaths In Local Jails: Factors Influencing Inmate Suicide.* Unpublished Masters Thesis. (Jackson, Mississippi: Jackson State University Library, 1995).
2. Ibid.

tors that have contributed to suicide attempts among African American inmates.

Particularly, Chapter5 presents a framework for examining those factors contributing to suicide attempts among African American inmates in Mississippi County jails. For instance, factors such as over crowding, deplorable conditions, and isolation have traditionally been variables examined regarding inmate suicide. However, these factors did not account for suicide among African American inmates in Mississippi county jails, other factors may explain suicide attempts among this group. To this end, several suppositions were postulated regarding suicide among African American inmates: It is suggested that the more an African American inmate's family expresses great care towards him, the less likely he will attempt suicide. It is proffered that the more likely an African American inmate is not a pre-trial detainee, the less likely he will attempt suicide. It is hypothesized that that if an African American inmate is a violent offender, then the less likely he will attempt suicide. It is further hypothesized that that if an African American inmate has been detained for more than 24 hours, he is less likely to attempt suicide. It is also suggested that if an African American inmate lacks a history of substance abuse, then he is less likely to attempt suicide. It is theorized that if an African American inmate lacks a history of previous arrests, then he is less likely to attempt suicide. It is proffered that if an African American inmate lacks low self-esteem, then he is less likely to attempt suicide.

Furthermore, the major research questions pondered within this chapter were(1) To what extent does family perception affect suicide attempts of an African American inmate?(2) To what extent does pre-trial detainee status affect suicide attempts among an African American inmate?(3) Does the type of offense committed by an African American inmate contribute to suicide attempts?(4) Does a history of substance abuse influence contribute to suicide attempts among African American inmates?(5) To what extent does a history of previous arrests influence suicide attempts of an African American inmate?(6) To what extent does the first 24 hours of incarceration contribute to suicide attempts among African American inmates?(7) and (8) To what extent does structural design of Mississippi jails contribute to attempted suicide among African American inmates? There has not been a plethora of literature examining attempted suicide among African American inmates in Mississippi county jails. However, this chapter at least in part, tries to generate a literature base by analyzing some of these aforementioned questions.

Specifically, from 1987 through 1993, 49 jail deaths have occurred in Mississippi county jails which all were reported as *suicide by hanging*. A face-to-face interview with African American civil rights activist and attorney, Chowke Lumumba, strongly felt that those jail deaths were not all *suicide*, but *homicide* committed by a corrupt police department.[3] Therefore, this chapter revisited those factors that lead to suicide attempts of African American inmates in Mississippi county jails. The section immediately following the introduction delineates available perspectives on inmate suicide. The next section provides a conceptual framework for understanding those factors that may influence or contribute to suicide attempts of African American inmates in Mississippi jails. The remaining half of this chapter delineates the research methodology and design of survey instrument that guided this study on suicide.

Available Perspectives on Inmate Suicide

First, the cultural disposition of African-Americans such as their natural innate nature to survive under tremendous pressure excludes this group from high rates of suicide within penal institutions. Because of African-Americans belief in God, mental strength, high spirituality, and high morals are virtues that have sustained this group as a racial minority when faced with life adversities. In particular, recent studies have shown that African-Americans are less likely to commit suicide within the general population compared with whites. For example, Peck and Colleagues (1985), they found that on average, whites commit suicide twice as often as African-Americans in the general population.[4]

No name is more closely associated with research in the area of jail and prison suicides than Lindsay Hayes. According to Hayes, suicide research in corrections has independently examined jail and prison populations.[5] The jail generally refers to local(city) and county detention facilities which hold individuals after arrest and who are awaiting trial or sentencing. Prisons, on the other hand, are usually state or federal facilities to which inmates are transferred after being sentenced for a conviction.[6] Jail detainees generally

---

3.   Chokwe Lumumba. Interview by Lisa Nikol Nealy. October 14, 1993(Jackson, Mississippi).
4.   Peck.
5.   Lindey Hayes. Jail standards and suicide prevention: another look.(Jail Mental Suicide Mental Update Volume 6:1-8, 1996).

are younger and are dealing with the initial stages of confinement, including arrest, the jail setting, and uncertainty regarding their legal process and outcome. Prisoners generally, on the other hand, are older than jail detainees, have had some time and experience in dealing with incarceration, and know the legal outcome of their arrest.[7] Historically, most attention has been given to the jail population in suicide research due to the critical nature of initial incarceration.

Hayes and his research team (through the National Center on Institutions and Alternatives) have conducted major national investigations on jail suicide. Beginning with the landmark study in 1981 and followed by its replication in 1986, Hayes et al. discovered an alarming suicide rate in jails throughout the country. The annual rate of suicide was found to be approximately 107 per 100,000 inmates; nine times higher than the rate for the general population. Further, research revealed a consistent profile for jail suicide victims: young, white, single, first-time arrest, non-violent offenders, intoxicated, substance abuse history, hanging by bed clothing, isolated jail housing, and death within the first 24 hours of arrest.[8]

Secondly, a national study of jail suicide conducted by the *National Center on Institutions Alternatives* (NCIA)(1981), documented that four hundred and nineteen suicides occurred in jails and lock up during 1979.[9] From the demographic data collected on 344 of these suicides, a profile of the typical victim was constructed. The suicide victim was most likely to be white, 72 percent; male 94 percent, mean age of the victim was thirty; single, 52 percent, detained on non-violent charges, 75 percent with 27 percent detained on alcohol drug related charges.[10] Also, the (NCIA) report found that 89 percent of the suicide victims were confined as detainees; 78 percent of the victims had prior charges; 60 percent of victims were intoxicated at the time of incarceration; over 50 percent of suicides occurred within the first 24-hours of incarceration; 94 percent of suicides were by hanging. Thirty percent of suicides occurred during a six-hour period between 12 midnight and 6 a.m. Eighty-nine percent of the suicide victims were not screened for potentially suicidal behavior at the time of booking.[11]

---

6.   Ibid.
7.   Ibid.
8.   http://www.igc.apc.org/ncia/spring2000update.htlm.
9.   Ibid.
10.   Ibid.
11.   Ibid.

Moreover, the design of jails has been brought into questions where the issue of suicide has occurred. Randy Atlas observed that the jail design and layout influence many jail suicides. For example, Atlas argued that the ability to adequately supervise and monitor jail inmates was greatly influenced by jail design and layout. Atlas also maintained that the American Correctional Association (ACA) showed that standard 3-ALDF-2C-01 required all general population cells and segregation cells 3-ALDF-2C-12 to provide a minimum of 80 square feet of which 35 square feet is unencumbered space.[12]

Research Methodology

The research methodology employed in this study is quantitative thus, numerical analysis is emphasized. The rest of this section entails a discussion of the various statistical tools utilized in this study.

A Framework for Studying Predictors of Suicide Attempts

The major theoretical framework in this study is based on Emiles Durkheim's suicide theory. Durkheim drew theoretical conclusions on the social causes of suicide. He proposed four types of suicide, based on the degrees of imbalance of two social forces: social integration and moral regulation. Durkheim placed emphasis on the structural forces that affect human behavior which causes suicide. I use Durkheim's suicide theory to explain attempted suicide among African American inmates. Specifically, the structural forces such as the design of Mississippi jails of deplorable conditions, overcrowdiness may lead to high attempts of suicide among African American inmates. Therefore, the major thesis statement is: As deplorable conditions of Mississippi jails decreases, suicide attempts among African American inmates decreases. Durkheim's theory was that suicide is related to the links people have with social groups. To little commitment to groups and group norms was likely to produce egoistic suicide. Too much was likely to produce altruistic suicide. Commitment shaken by rapid social change was likely to increase the chances of anomic suicide (Durkheim 2003: durkheim.ito).

---

12.   Randy Atlas. Reducing the opportunity for inmate suicide:a design guide(Psychiatric Quarterly 60, 1989), 161-171.

Figure 2.4: A Model of Suicide-Attempts and Non-Attempts, 2003.

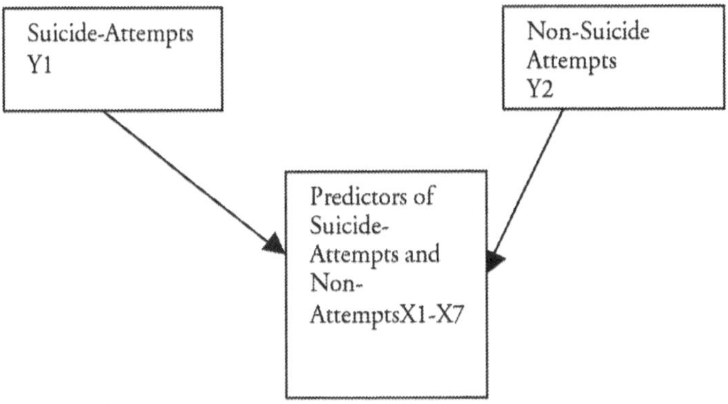

This model provides a framework for explicating attempted suicides and non-attempts of African American inmates in Mississippi County Jails. This model simply describes partial causes that influence some inmates to attempt suicide tested against those non-attempters. The relationship assumed in this model is to distill some of the important independent variables explored by social scientists within the criminal justice literature. The major independent variables represented by X were family perception, awaiting trial, offense committed, length of confinement, previous arrest, substance abuse, and self-perception. The dichotomous dependent variable is represented by Y which implies that there exist two categorical variables—those inmates who attempted suicide and those who did not. The basic supposition derived from this model is that African American inmates are less likely to attempt suicide when the conditions of Mississippi county jails are not deplorable. I expect to find that African American inmates are less likely to attempt suicide when their family cares a great deal about them, awaiting trail, non-violent offense, no prior arrests, no history of alcohol and drug abuse, and no self-esteem issues. Excluding the importance of specific predictors of suicide attempts in this model is quite difficult both theoretically and empirically because every inmate incarcerated is at risk of attempting suicide. Therefore, I sought empirical confirmation of these variables enumerated in the model by testing seven hypotheses. These hypotheses are stated below.

Hypotheses

In this study, seven hypotheses undergird this research:

H_1: The more positive a family's perception is towards an African American inmate, the less likely he is to attempt suicide?

H_2: The more likely an African American inmate is not awaiting trial, the less likely he will attempt suicide.

H_3: If an African American inmate is not a non-violent offender, the less likely he will attempt suicide.

H_4: If an African American inmate has been incarcerated more than 24 hours, then he will less likely attempt suicide.

H_5: If an African American inmate does not have a history of substance abuse, then he will less likely attempt suicide.

H_6: The more likely an African American inmate has no history of previous arrests, he will less likely attempt suicide.

H_7: The more likely an African American inmate's self-esteem is positive, he will less likely attempt suicide.

Research Design

The research design in this study is based on a multivariate data analysis. The multivariate data analysis included the following statistical techniques: Cross-Tabs, Discriminant Analysis and Analysis of Variance (ANOVA). The primary data source used in this analysis is a 38-item survey instrument that consisted of open-ended questions. Each survey item was encoded using an advance statistical software program called, Statistical Program for Social Scientists (SPSS. 10). Therefore, the results produced in this study are derived from these SPSS program runs.

Operationalization of Variables

There are a total of seven major independent variables(i.e., family perception, awaiting trial, offense charged with, length of confinement, previous arrests, substance abuse and self-esteem) and one dichotomous dependent variable (attempted suicide) tested in this study. Secondary independent variables like deplorable conditions, overcrowdness, and isolation are measured in the ANOVA to test for significance since the original inmate study found these variables statistically insignificant. These variables are operationalized as follows:

(1)Family Perception-(Independent Variable)—This measure was operationalized to the extent that an African American inmate's family expresses a positive perception which can decrease attempts at suicide. Ordinal is the level of measurement for this variable.

(2)Awaiting Trial (Independent Variable)-This measure was operationalized as those African American inmates whom was either pre-trial detainee waiting to be tried and already convicted. Awaiting trial is a key determinant in predicting attempts at suicide of inmates in general. Nominal is the level of measurement for this variable.

(3)Offense Charged With (Independent Variable)-This measure was operationalized to the extent that those African American inmates' offense is identified as non-violent or violent. Offense charged with is more likely to determine whether an inmate attempts suicide. Ordinal is the level of measurement.

(4)Length of Confinement(Independent Variable)-This measure was operationalized as those African American inmates who are detained for 24 hours or more. Ordinal is the level of measurement for this variable. Length of confinement has also been a strong predictor of attempted inmate suicide in jails.

(5)Previous Arrest (Independent Variable)—This measure was opertionalized as those African American inmates who had been arrested one or more times that influences their attempts at suicide. Nominal is the level of measurement for this variable.

(6)Substance Abuse (Independent Variable)-This measure was operationalized as those African American inmates who had a history of drugs or alcohol abuse before becoming incarcerated. Nominal is the level of measurement for this variable.

(7)<u>Self-Esteem</u> (Independent Variable)-This measure was opertaionalized to the extent by which those African American inmates' self-esteem ranges from high to low in contributing to their attempts at suicide.

(8)<u>Attempted</u> <u>Suicide</u> (Dichotomous Dependent Variable One)—This measure was operationalized to the extent those African American inmates had attempted suicide while detained or already convicted. Nominal is the level of measurement for this variable.

(9.)<u>Non-Attempted</u> <u>Suicide</u> (Dichotomous Dependent Variable Two)-This measure was operationalized to the extent those African American inmates had not attempted suicide while detained or already convicted.

Data Collection

There were 50 or more detainees chosen voluntarily from each of the four jail populations. The research instrument used in this study was a 38-item structured survey. The population was to include Alcorn County Jail, Forrest County Jail, and Jones Correctional Detention Center for Adults, Simpson County Jails, and Hinds County Jail. Five of these Mississippi local county jails are cited by the U.S. Justice Department as the worst jail facilities to house any human. Hinds County Jail was selected based on location and accessibility. The procedure for collecting data was random sampling. In this study, a total of 264 inmates were voluntarily selected from Jones Correctional Adult Detention Center, Lauderdale County Jail, Simpson County Jail, and Hinds County Jail. Every inmate was given a chance to participate in the survey interviews at each jail. Either these inmates were pre-trialed detainees(awaiting trial) or convicted inmates (those already tried and sentenced). The sample required a number of 50 or more from the four jail populations; however, only Lauderdale and Hinds met this number. There was also a cross-section of inmates both pre-trial and convicted who were surveyed. An increase in female incarceration rates resulted in more females surveyed compared to the original study.

Data Analysis

Discriminant analysis was the best statistical technique to employ because the dependent variable was dichotomous and categorical(e.g. Attempted suicide vs. non-attempted suicide). The objective of this statistic was to produce the variable(s) that yielded the highest discriminating power with attempted suicide. Those variables that scored the highest ranging from 0.99 to a low of 0.55 became greater predictors of attempted suicide. Cross-Tabs were used on specific items on the survey that pertained to social characteristics of the suicidal inmate or those inmates who attempted suicide in order to show comparisons with non-African American inmates. The social characteristics included marital status, age, parent's history of abuse, number of children inmate had, history of substance abuse, and method used to attempt suicide. Out of 246 inmates surveyed, 29 had attempted suicide.

Analysis of Variance (ANOVA) was utilized because we wanted to test for the explained variance of each independent variable against the dependent variable. ANOVA was used to test for statistical differences between the dichotomous dependent variable and independent variables. Thus, the alpha level used to test for significance was .05.

Results

This section describes the results generated from the survey interviews conducted in 1999. It should be noted that selected results are given from the original study conducted in 1995 on inmates in Mississippi county jails. These results are important to describe because they reflect a comparative analysis from 1995 to 1999. Selected tables and figures are shown here from the 1995 study that revealed the following: The mean score and standard deviations were used to test for any distinct differences or variation in both these groups. Group I was comprised of those inmates who had attempted suicide. Group II was those inmates who had not attempted suicide. The sample was derived from Hinds County Jail, Jones County Jail, and Forrest County Jail.

Table 1-11. Classification Analysis of Dichotomous Dependent Variable for Attempters of Suicide—GROUP I, 1995.

CONTROL FACTORS	$\overline{X}$ (MEAN)	S(STANDARD DEVIATION)	N(TOTAL NUMBER OF CASES)
Family Perception	1.00	-----	11
Awaiting Trial	1.33	-----	11
Offense Charged	4.66	------	11
Length of Confinement	1.00	------	11

Table 1-11. Classification Analysis of Dichotomous Dependent Variable for Attempters of Suicide—GROUP I, 1995. (Continued)

CONTROL FACTORS	X̄ (MEAN)	S(STANDARD DEVIATION)	N(TOTAL NUMBER OF CASES)
Previous Arrest	1.33	------	11
History of Substance Abuse	1.66	---------	11
Self Perception	2.01	---------	11

DATA SOURCE: Data taken from the 1994 Jail Inmate Suicide Study.

Table 1-11. depicts Group I that comprised those inmates who attempted suicide. There were a total of 11 inmates out of 143 from the three local Mississippi County Jails who had attempted suicide. The control factors ranged from family perception to self-esteem in which the mean scores and standard deviations were computed. The mean scores for family perception was a 1.00 which suggests that on average, those inmates who attempted suicide were more likely to have family who cared very little about them. In Group II (see Table 1-12.), the mean score for family perception of the non-attempters was a 1.33 which suggest that on average, those inmates who did not attempt suicide were more likely to have family that cared about their well-being.

Table 1-12. Classification Analysis of Dichotomous Dependent Variable for Non-Attempters of Suicide-GROUP II, 1995.

CONTROL FACTORS	X̄ (Mean)	S(standard deviation)	N (TOTAL NUMBER OF CASES)
Family Perception	1.33	-----	11
Awaiting Trial	2.00	-----	11
Offense Charged	5.00	-----	11
Length of Confinement	1.33	-----	11
Previous Arrest	1.00	-----	11
History of Substance Abuse	1.33	--------	11
Self-Perception	2.66	--------	11

DATA SOURCE: DATA Derived from the 1995 Jail Inmate Suicide Study (Nealy 1995).

The mean score for the non-attempters of suicide for alcohol abuse was 1.66; mean score for drug abuse was 1.33; mean score for previous arrest was 1.00; offense charge with had a mean score of 5.00; mean score fore awaiting trial was 2.00; mean score for self-esteem was 2.66; mean score for length of confinement was 1.33; and mean score for family perception was 1.33.

The mean score for those inmates who attempted suicide (Group I) was greater than those non-attempters (Group II) of suicide for drug abuse. This score suggests that those inmates who attempted suicide had a higher occurrence of drug abuse than those inmates who had not attempted suicide.

Furthermore, a profile of the typical inmate housed in the three Mississippi County Jails is delineated in Table 1.13.

Table 1.13. Profile of Typical Inmate in Mississippi County Jails, Forrest, Jones, and Hinds, 1995.

STATUS OF INMATE	PRE-TRIAL DETAINEE (48.6)
RACE/ETHNICITY	AFRICAN-AMERICAN (75.4%)
GENDER	MALE (81.8%)
AGE	17years old
EDUCATIONAL LEVEL	HIGH SCHOOL GRADUATES (55%)
TYPE OF CRIME	NON-VIOLENT

This table is a profile of the typical inmate in Mississippi county jails detained in 1995 (Nealy 1994). The typical inmate in the Mississippi county jails in 1995 was African-American males, a total of 75.4 percent and male, 81.8 percent. The next table illustrates the typical inmate who attempted suicide in Mississippi County Jails in 1995.

The next table described the jail demographics of inmate population from the four Mississippi County Jails of Lauderdale, Hinds, Jones, and Simpson.

Table 1-14. Jail Demographics of Inmates in Mississippi County Jails, Lauderdale, Hinds, Jones, and Simpson, 2001.

RACE	N	TOTAL
African-American	155	58.7%
White	96	36.4%
Hispanic	6	2.3%
Other	2	.8%
GENDER		
Female	96	36.4%
Male	167	63.3%
AGE	264	100%
16-19yrs.	female, male	
20	male	
21-24	female, male	
25-28	female, male	
29-32	female, male	
33-34	female, male	
35	male	
36-39	female, male	
40	male	
41-43	female, male	
44	female	
45-46	female, male	
50-59	female, male	
EDUCATIONAL LEVEL		
Less than high school	80	30%
High School	119	45.1%
Less than College	35	13.3%
College Graduate	22	8.3%
Beyond 4yrs College	4	1.5%
COUNTY JAILS		
Lauderdale	117	44.3%
Hinds	83	31.4%
Jones	39	14.8%
Simpson	25	9.5%

DATA SOURCE: Results generated from SPSS Program Runs of a 38-item self-study survey, 1999.

From the above table, there were a total of 264 inmates surveyed in this study in 1999. The sample size was larger than the sample population surveyed in 1994 with only 143 respondents due to restrictions of jail access. Another noticeable trend from this jail demographic of 1999 compared to 1994 demographics was the increase in female inmates' incarceration rates. Eighteen point two percent were interviewed in 1994 compared to 36.4 percent of female inmates in 1999 This increase in female inmates has been visible throughout the general penal institutions across the United States. The youngest inmate surveyed was 16 years of age while the oldest was 59 years. I also found that those inmates interviewed in 1999 had completed high school at much higher rates than in 1994. Forty-five percent of the inmates interviewed in 1999 had completed high school compared to only 38.5 percent in 1994. The largest inmate population interviewed came from Lauderdale County Jail with a total of 117. Hinds County jail population was 83 inmates while Jones County Adult Detention Correctional Facility had 39 inmates who participated in the survey interview. Simpson County Jail population had the smallest samples with only 25 inmates surveyed.

Table 1-12. Structure Matrix of Discriminating Variables and Canonical Functions, 1999.

DISCRIMINATING VARIABLES	CANONICAL FUNCTION
Offense Charged with	0.524
History of Substance Abuse	0.522
Self-Perception	0.487
Previous Arrest	-0.240
Length of Confinement	0.180
Family Perception	0.121
Awaiting Trial	0.098

DATA SOURCE: Results Generated From SPSS Program Runs of a 38-item self-study survey, 1999.

In the above table, offense charged with had the largest discriminating function with the dependent variable, attempted suicide. History of substance abuse showed the second highest discriminating function with attempted suicide. Previous arrest as a discriminating variable showed a negative score, which indicates that there exist some correlations with, attempted suicide. In other words, those inmates who indicated that they had attempted suicide also had been arrested more than one time. The least discriminating variable was the inmates awaiting trial because it had the smallest correlation with inmates who attempted suicide.

Moreover, the sample mean or group centroid was utilized to describe differences between those inmates who attempted suicide from the non-attempters of suicide. In order to measure the influence of one variable, it was important to analyze those predicted independent variables controlled for attempted suicide. Group I and Group II represent the two dependent or dichotomous variables identified as "attempters of suicide" vs. "non-attempters of suicide".

The sample population was taken from four Mississippi County Jails that included Lauderdale, Hinds, Jones Adult Correctional Facility, and Simpson County respectively. For instance, Group—I had a total of 29 inmates that attempted suicide compared to Group II. In Group-II, a total of 231 had not attempted suicide. Thus, there were a total of 260 cases used in this analysis. Those inmates who had attempted suicide were more likely to be placed in isolation than the non-attempters. Below, Tables 1.13 and Table 1.13a reflect the analysis based on the mean scores and standard deviations.

Table 1-13. Classification Analysis of Dichotomous Dependent Variable Attempted Suicide/Group-I, 1999.

CONTROL FACTORS	X̄ (MEAN)	S(STANDARD DEVIATION)	N(TOTAL NUMBER OF CASES)
Family Perception	1.379	1.115%	29
Awaiting Trial	1.344	.768%	29
Offense Charged	4.137	2.416%	29
Length of Confinement	1.131	1.574%	29
Previous Arrest	1.379	.493%	29
History of Substance Abuse	1.413	.501%	29
Self-Perception	1.724	1.61%	29

Data Source: Results Generated From SPSS program Runs of a 38-item self-study survey, 1999.

Table 1.14. Classification Analysis of Dichotomous Dependent Variable
Non—Attempts/Group-II, 1999.

CONTROL FACTORS	X̄(MEAN)	S(STANDARD DEVIATION)	N(TOTAL NUMBER OF CASES)
Family Perception	1.480	.968%	231
Awaiting Trial	1.398	.623%	231
Offense Charged	4.935	1.704	231
Length of Confinement	1.359	1.431%	231
Previous Arrests	1.277	.503%	231
History of Substance Abuse	1.632	.492%	231
Self-Perception	2.190	1.126%	231

DATA SOURCE: Results Generated From SPSS Program Runs of a 38-item self-study survey, 1999.

In Table 1-13, the mean score for family perception was 1.379 and the standard deviation was 1.115 for Group I, the attempters of suicide; however, the mean score fore this same variable in Group II, non-attempters of suicide was a 1.480 and the standard deviation a .968 percent. This mean score for Group I was less than the mean score for Group II which suggest that on average, those inmates who attempted suicide in Group I indicated that their family cared very little about them compared to those inmates representing Group II. Here, family perception had the largest difference in standard deviation scores (1.11percent vs. .96percent) which indicated a small variation on this variable. The total number of inmates from Group I who had attempted suicide was 29 while a total of 231 inmates from Group II had not attempted suicide.

The mean score for those awaiting trial in Group I was a 1.344 and standard deviation ranged as .76 percent while the mean score for this same control factor in Group II was a 1.398 with a standard deviation of .62percent. The mean score for Group I was less than the mean score for Group II which suggest that on average, those inmates who had attempted suicide were more likely to be pre-trial detainees than those from Group II. The mean score for Group II suggest that there were a greater number of non-attempters of suicide who had already been convicted. Here, awaiting trial showed a small difference in standard deviation scores (.76percent vs.62percent) which suggest very little variation on this variable.

The mean score for offense charged with in Group I, Table 1.13 was a 4.137 and in Group II, Table 1.14 showed a mean score for this same variable as 4.935. The mean score for offense charged with in Group I indicates that on average, those inmates who had attempted suicide were charged with less violent offenses than those non-attempter inmates from Group II. The non-attempters from Group II were more likely to be charged with violent crimes based on the mean score of 4.935. Here, offense charged with had the largest difference in standard deviation scores (2.41percent vs.1.70percent) which suggest a high variation on this variable.

The mean score of length of confinement for Group I was 1.37 and 1.359 for Group II. These mean scores suggest that on average, those inmates who attempted suicide had longer lengths of confinement than the non-attempters, however; the literature review suggested that those suicidal inmates were more likely to have been held in custody less than twenty-four hours. Thus, this mean score on this particular variable is partially inconsistent with the literature. Length of confinement had a small difference in standard deviation scores of (1.57percent vs. 1.43percent) which suggest that there was little variation on this variable.

The mean score of Group I was 1.379 and 1.277 for Group II for the variable previous arrests. These mean scores suggest that on average, those inmates who attempted suicide had more arrests than the non-attempters of suicide. Previous arrests had standard deviation scores of (.49percent vs. 50percent) which suggest that there was a very small difference in variation on this variable between both groups. In addition, the mean score for history of substance abuse was 1.413 for Group I and 1.632 for Group II. These scores indicated that on average, those inmates who attempted suicide had less history of substance abuses than the non-attempters. This score is inconsistent with the literature review regarding substance abuse and those inmates prone to suicide. The literature review averred that those inmates who are prone to suicide were more likely to have higher incidence of substance abuse (i.e., alcohol, drug, painkillers,). The mean score for self-perception of Group I was 1.724 and 2.190 of Group II. These scores indicate that on average, those inmates who attempted suicide had a much lower self-esteem than the non-attempters. Here, self-perception had a moderate, but no large difference in standard deviation scores (1.16percent vs. 1.12percent).

Furthermore, another statistical technique employed in this study was ANOVA (i.e., Analysis of Variance) to test for statistical differences between the dichotomous dependent variables and independent variables. In other words, ANOVA explains the variance or variability of each grouped variable. Figure 2.5 below describes in more detail the explained variance of factors influencing suicide among jail inmates.

Figure 2.5: Explained Variance In Attempted Suicide of Mississippi Jail Inmates, 1999.

Variables	Wilks Lambda	F-Statistics	Degree of Freedom	Degree of Freedom	Level of Significant
Family Perception	.99	.272	1	258	.603**
Awaiting Trial	.99	.179	1	258	.672**
Offense Charge	.98	5.08	1	258	.025*
Length of Confine	.99	.603	1	258	.438**
Previous Arrest	.99	1.06	1	258	.302**
History of Substance Abuse	.98	5.045	1	258	.026*
Self-Perception	.98	4.38	1	258	.037*
Deplorable	.99	1.92	1	258	.166**
Overcrowd-edness	.99	.207	1	258	.649**
Isolation	.98	2.81	1	258	.094**

DATA SOURCE: Results generated from the SPSS Program based on a 38-item self-study survey 1999. $p = <0.05*$ is statistically significant; $p > 0.05**$ is statistically insignificant.

In Figure 2.4, only three of these predictor variables showed a statistical difference when measured at alpha level of 0.05. If the observed significance was 5 percent or less, the variable was considered significant and accepted the hypothesis. However, if the observed significance was higher than 5 percent then it was not significant to accept the hypothesis was rejected. Offense charged with had an observed significance of .02(p<0.05) which suggested that this variable was statistically significant with attempted suicide of inmates. History of substance abuse had an observed significance of .026(p<0.05) which indicated that this variable also was statistically significant with attempted suicide of inmates. Also, Self-perception showed an observed significance of .037(p<0.05) which suggested that this variable was statistically significant with attempted suicide of jail inmates. Conversely, family perception, awaiting trial, length of confinement, previous arrest, all had significant levels greater than p>0.05 which were not statistically significant with attempted suicide of jail inmates. The three original independent variables tested in the original inmate suicide study such as deplorable conditions, overcrowded, and isolation resulted in statistically insignificant observed scores with attempted suicide. Again, these variables all had observed significance sores greater than p.>0.05 probability level that rendered them statistically insignificant with attempted suicide.

The F value for offense charge with was 5.08; history of substance abuse 5.04, and self-perception 4.38 reflected the total variability of each of these grouped variables in explaining attempted suicide of jail inmates. Each of these F-value scores suggest that there was an equal variance for offense charged and history of substance abuse with attempted suicide, but self-perception F-value reflected a partial variance with attempted suicide. In addition, the Lambda (reliability score measured in percent) scores for offenses charge with (.98percent), history of substance abuse,(.98percent) and self-perception (.98%) measured at a reliability score of .98percent. This score suggested that each of these three variables were 98percent reliable in explaining the strength of association with the dichotomous dependent variable, attempted suicide. Although the other predictor variables such as family perception, awaiting trial, length of confinement, and previous arrest showed a .99 percent of reliability in explaining the strength of association with attempted suicide, their level of significance scores statistically failed to correlate with attempted suicide. Lastly, the first degrees of freedom for all seven predictor variables was a 1 which suggested that the sampling distribution of those inmates who attempted suicide in this study were less skewed.

While the second degrees of freedom ranged was a 258 illuminates the sampling distribution of those inmates who were non-attempters of suicide were more skewed.

Most important, the Summary statistic reflects the totality of my model tested in this study based on the dichotomous dependent variables (i.e., Attempted suicide vs. Non-attempters of suicide). The summary statistics is the final score in which the researcher determines whether the data fits the theory based on the results produced. However, if results from the foregoing summary statistics yield different results, then replication of the original study will be obsolete. Below, Figure 2.6 depicts the summary statistics of the overall model.

Figure 2.6: Summary Statistics of Canonical Discriminant Functions, 2001.

Dichotomous Dependent Variables(Test of Functions)	Wilks' Lambda	Chi-Square	Degree of Freedom	Level of Significance
1	.933	17.523	10	.064

DATA SOURCE: Results Generated From SPSS Program Runs of a 38-item self-study survey, 1999.

In Figure 2.6, the dichotomous dependent variables are indicated by a function of 1. In particular, when the number of groups are two, i.e., attempted suicide vs. non-attempts, there's only one canonical variable to consider. In this vein, Wilks' Lamda score of .93 indicated that 93 % of the total variance in the discriminant score was not explained by group differences. Lambda was thus transformed to a variable with an approximated chi-square distribution. The chi-square was a score of 17.523 which indicated a very low significant difference between the two group centroids. Because the observed significance level was .06(p>0.05) greater than .05, the model failed to fit the data.

Figure 2.7: Typology I-Composite of the Typical Inmate in Mississippi
County Jails, 1999.

Status of Inmate	Pre-trial detainee (59%)
Race/Ethnicity	African American (59.8%)
Gender	Male (63.3%)
Age	30 years old (6.8%)
Type of Crime	Non-Violent (56.8%)
Educational Level	High School Graduate (45.1%)

DATA SOURCE: Results generated from Jail Inmate Suicide Study (Nealy 1999).

The above figure depicts a profile of the typical inmate in Mississippi County jails from Lauderdale, Hinds, Jones Correctional Adult Detention Facility, and Simpson County Jails. These results generated from the data on jail inmate suicide in 1999 differ from the type of inmate house in Mississippi County Jails in 1994. One of the largest changes in the typical inmate population from Mississippi County Jails in 1999 was their age. The mean age of the typical inmate in 1999 was much older than the typical inmate housed in 1994. (see page 62.) The mean age was 30 years old in 1999 from the mean age of 17 in 1994. There was a decrease in the male inmate population housed in 1999 with a total of 63.3 percent than in 1994 ranging at 81.8 percent. The changing trend in the 1999 study of inmate population was the increase in female inmates entering the penal system in Mississippi county jails. The type of crime committed by the typical inmate housed in Mississippi County jails in 1999 were non-violent with 56.8 percent ranging from driving under the influence (DUI), child-support, shoplifting, to violating parole and possession of drugs. In 1994, the percentage of non-violent offense committed by inmates from Mississippi County Jails was 11.8 percent differences. Figure 2.8 depicts the profile of a typical suicidal inmate in Mississippi County Jails.

Figure 2.8: Typology II-Profile of Typical Suicidal Inmate in Mississippi
County Jails, 1999.

Status of Inmates	Pre-trial detainee
Race/ethnicity	White
Gender	Male
Age	19
Type of Offense Committed	Non-violent
Lock-Down Status	Isolation
Educational Level	High school graduate

Data Source: Data Taken from 1999 Jail Inmate Suicide Study Survey(Nealy,1999).

Figure 2.8 represents the profile of an inmate who is likely to attempt suicide in Mississippi County Jails. The profile of the typical suicidal inmate is white, male, and 19 years of age. The status of these typical inmates is one of pre-trial detainee who was awaiting trial for a non-violent offense and placed in isolation. These inmates who had attempted suicide were high school graduates. Not shown in this figure is that the same number of African American inmates (14) had reported attempts of suicide as well; however, white inmates are more likely to attempt suicide and succeed. Figure 2.8b illustrates the social characteristics of these inmates who had attempted suicide.

Figure 2.8b: Social Profile of Inmates Who Attempted Suicide in Mississippi County Jails, 1999.

Marital Status	Single
Children	Yes
History of Sexual Abuse	Yes
History of Drug Abuse	Yes
Marital Status of Parents	Married
History of Violence Between Parents	Yes
History of Parent Abuse	Yes
Attempts of Suicide	Yes
Method Used in Attempts of Suicide	Hanging
Self-Esteem	Somewhat Satisfied

DATA SOURCE: Results Generated From SPSS Cross-tabs derived from 1999 Jail Data on Inmate Suicide (Nealy, 1999).

Figure 2.8b shows the social profile of those inmates who had a history of attempts at suicide. Those inmates who had attempted suicide indicated that they were single. A total number of twenty-five (25) indicated that they had children while three (3) of the inmates did not have none. Twelve of the suicidal inmates indicated that their parents sexually abused them. Seventeen of the inmates had a history of drug abuse. Seven of the inmate's parents were married. Fourteen of the suicidal inmates had witnessed violence between their parents. Thirteen of the inmates indicated that their parents had been abusive towards them. A total of twenty-nine inmates indicated they had attempted suicide. Ten of the inmates stated that the method used to commit suicide was by hanging while eight of the inmates did not respond to this question. These social characteristics of the inmates who had attempted suicide grew up in homes that were unstable and very dysfunctional.

Moreover, figure 2.10 depicts the design of Mississippi County Jails in Lauderdale County, Hinds County, Jones Correctional Adult Detention Facility, and Simpson County. The basic design or condition of these four Mississippi county jails played a key role in contributing to inmates attempting suicide. Th design of the jail was based on two criterions: 1. Adequate Conditions-when the jail meets the general standards of a jail set forth by the ACA that includes but not limited to sufficient beds, sufficient cell space, sanitary environment within the cell, and sufficient amount of jail staff and 2. Inadequate-when the jail fails to meet basic standards set forth by the ACA that includes inmates exceeding the number of beds, unsanitary cell dwellings, insufficient amount of cell space, and lack of trained staff. It should be noted that even if a jail meets the general standards of adequate facility does not necessarily rule out the probability of attempted suicides occurring.

Figure 2.9: Typology III-The Profile and Design of Mississippi's County Jails in Lauderdale, Hinds, Jones Correctional Adult Detention Facility, and Simpson, 1999.

Name of County Jail	Non-Inmate Population*	Racial-Make-up of General population*	*Per Capita Income	City of County Jails	Design of County Jails**
Lauderdale	76,910	Non-white-26,280;white-48,706	17,782	Merid-ian	Adequate***
Hinds	251,031	Non-white-129,591;white-123,179	49,601	Jackson	Adequate
Jones	63,001	Nonwhite-15,495;white-46,151	16,059	Laurel	Adequate***
Simpson	25,144	Nonwhite-7,737;white-16,124	15,224	Men-denhall	Inadequate***

DATA SOURCE: *Mississippi Statistical Abstract (1998). **Derived from personal visit to jail facility and interviewing jail administrators in (Nealy face-to-face interviews 1995; b.1999). *** Jail was ordered to upgrade to adequate standards by the U.S. Justice Department(Janet Reno Report on Mississippi Jails 1995).

The non-inmate cell refers to the general population. The racial make-up refers to the general racial composition of the general population and the average income level that specific county. The next cell identifies the name of the city where the county jail is located. The last cell describes the structural condition of each county jail. For example, Lauderdale County Jail located in Meridian, Mississippi. The non-inmate population is 76,910 where the racial composition is majority white. The average income level of the general populace is about seven-teen thousand, seven hundred and eighty-two dollars. The structural condition of Lauderdale County Jail in 1999 was adequate. This county jail was a newly built jail as a result of Reno's recommendations for jail officials and administrators of Lauderdale County Jail to upgrade its facility. In 1994, Reno declared this jail inadequate because of severe overcrowding and deplorable conditions. A number of suicides have occurred in the Lauderdale County Jail prior to the upgrade. While there wasn't any inmate suicides reported since the upgrade, many of them had attempted suicide by hanging.

Hinds County Jail is located in Jackson, Mississippi. The non-inmate population is 251, 031 people reside. The racial composition is majority African-American. The average income of Jackson's populace is forty-nine thousand, six hundred and one dollar. Hinds County Jail was considered adequate. This jail has no history of suicide but a history of attempted suicides by hanging.

Jones County Jail now called Jones Correctional Adult Detention Center, is located in Laurel, Mississippi. The non-inmate population of Laurel Mississippi is estimated at sixty-three thousand. The racial composition of Laurel Mississippi is majority white. The average income of Laurel's resident is sixteen thousand and fifty-nine dollars. The structural conditions or design of the Jones Correctional Adult Detention Center was deemed adequate as a result of its upgrade. Prior to its upgrade to the new facility, Reno cited Jones County Jail as inadequate because of the severe deplorable conditions in 1994. Before the new jail facility was built, the old Jones County Jail had a history of suicides. In 1999, the inmates that were surveyed indicated attempts at suicide by hanging.

Simpson County Jail is located in Mendenhall, Mississippi where the non-inmate population is 25, 144. The racial make-up is majority white. The average income of the populace is $15,224 dollars. Simpson County Jail was deemed inadequate. This jail has a history of suicide by hanging. The inmates surveyed in 1999 indicated that they had attempted suicide by hanging.

Findings

The goal was to test which variables had the highest discriminating power with attempted suicide and non-attempts. Seven variables were controlled for assumed to affect the dichotomous dependent variables in question. There were <u>seven</u> hypotheses that undergirded this study. Hypothesis1: Does family perception contribute to inmate suicide? Hypothesis 1 .603(p>0.05) was rejected because family perception was not statistically significant with attempted suicide. Hypothesis 2: Does awaiting trial contribute to inmate suicide? Hypothesis 2 was rejected .672(p>0.05) because those inmates awaiting trial or pre-trial detainee was not statistically significant with attempted suicide. Hypothesis 3: Does the length of confinement contribute to inmate suicide? Hypothesis 3 .438(p>0.05) was rejected because length of confinement did not statistically correlate with inmate suicide. Hypothesis 4: Does a history of previous arrests contribute to inmate suicide? Hypothesis 4 .302(p>0.05) was rejected because previous arrests did not statistically correlate with attempted suicide. Whether an inmate has been incarcerated more than once did not influence him/her to attempt suicide.

Even more, Hypothesis 5: Does offence committed influence inmate suicide? Hypothesis 5 .025(p>0.05) was accepted because non-violent offenses were statistically significant with attempted suicide. Hypothesis 6: Does a history of substance contribute to inmate suicide? I also failed to reject hypothesis 6 because history of alcohol and drug abuse of the inmate was statistically correlated with inmate suicide. Hypothesis 7: Does low self-esteem contributes to inmate suicide? I also failed to reject hypothesis 7 .037(p>0.05) because low self-perception was statistically significant with attempted suicide.

These findings suggest two conceptual realities of Mississippi county jail inmates: (1)When the structural conditions or design of the jail is adequate, the less likely an African American inmate will attempt suicide and succeed. (2) When the status of the typical inmate is not a first time offender, been confine more than twenty four hours, no history of substance abuse, and sense of self esteem he is less likely to attempt suicide. However, those independent variables that showed a high correlation with the dependent dichotomous variable-attempted suicide were offense charge with, history of substance abuse and self-esteem.

These findings also suggest that white inmates were more likely to attempt suicide than African American inmates and Hispanics. These findings are consistent with the literature and previous studies conducted on jail inmate suicide. What remains an anomaly is the number of African American jail inmates incarcerated in Mississippi county jails that have become victims to attempts at suicide by hanging. The empirical studies conducted by Hayes and others maintained that the white young males were more likely to attempt and succeed at suicide compared with African American inmates.

These findings raise questions about isolation, family perception awaiting trial, length of confinement and previous arrests used in earlier studies to explain inmate suicide in local jails. Several theories have been advanced which suggest that deplorable conditions, overcrowdedness, and isolation have been factors influencing inmate suicide in local jails (Wooldregde and Winfre 1992; Cohen and Gobert 1981; Liebling 1992; Winkler 1992; Palmer 1973). Secondly awaiting trial, length of confinement, and previous arrests, have also been cited as strong predictors of jail inmate suicide (Dooley 1987; Grover 1878; Hayes 1989;).

Conclusions

Based on the hypotheses and testing of Durkheim's theory of suicide, these findings are valid because this study actually measured what was intended to be measured. Also, this study is reliable because it provided consistent and accurate results. Those factors tested that believed to be the causes of attempted suicide among African American inmates were consistent with findings from the initial study conducted in 1995. Those findings suggested that more than social factors accounted for the attempted suicides among inmates in Mississippi jails which are consistent with the current findings. The current findings suggested that the design of the Mississippi jails can account for a high rate of attempted suicide among African American inmates. The design of Mississippi jails being deplorable, inadequate jail staff, and foul play) resulted in a high rate of attempted suicide among African American inmates. These findings have also shed light on those structural factors that contributed to inmates attempting suicide. What is also evident from these findings is that the majority of those inmates who attempted suicide were white. Because most of the inmates were white that reported attempts at suicide, this raises a level of suspicion as to why African

American male inmates indicated they had attempted suicide as well. Such findings have significant impact within the African American community and on public policy. The African American community in Mississippi doubts that all 24 hanging deaths of African American male inmates were suicide. Foul play by Mississippi jail administrators who were responsible for these deaths were never brought to trial for these lynching. And to date, there hasn't been any systematic effort of African American State legislators to pass some type of jail legislation that protects African American inmates from becoming victims of *lynching* inside Mississippi county jails.

Finally, these salient findings allow for generalizations to be made regarding the inmates incarcerated within Mississippi County Jails. First and foremost, the typical suicidal inmate incarcerated within Lauderdale County, Hinds County, Jones Correctional Adult Detention Center, and Simpson County, was white, young and male. Secondly, a disproportionate number of inmates incarcerated in these jails were African Americans who were likely to attempt suicide compared to white inmates. African American inmates' cultural disposition excludes them from not only attempting suicide but also succeeding. In addition, the design of most Mississippi County Jails is inadequate for any human to be housed. Thirdly, African American inmates who died by "hanging" in 1987 to 1994 inside of Mississippi's county jails were simply murdered the 'ole' fashion way—"LYNCHED". Mississippi county jail officers, sheriffs, have refuted the claims that they are completely responsible for not preventing the hanging deaths of African American inmates and non-African American inmates housed in their jail facilities from 1987 to 1993 and 1993 to date. However, the findings from my 1995 and 1999 data revealed otherwise. Inferences can be implicitly drawn from these findings that suggest sociological and psychological factors were not the only indicators which influenced African American inmates to attempt suicide by hanging. Indeed, these findings lead to the conclusion that it is highly unlikely that those African American inmates who were found with their throat and larynx muscles missing, body bruised, and dead bodies hanging from their jail cells, killed themselves. They were simply lynched.

COMMENTS AND
OBSERVATIONS

There were complexities involved in gaining access to these jail populations in Mississippi because of my gender and race. Being African American and female played a dual role in me gaining access to only 3 of 6 targeted Mississippi local jails in 1993. In 1999, I was allowed into 4 of the 6 Mississippi local jails that were the same six initially targetd in 1993. I also had to submit written documents to those Mississippi Jail administrators such as the Sheriff and Chief of Police who granted me access to their facility.

First, the original study conducted in 1993 was restricted to the three jails in Mississippi(i.e., Hinds, Jones, and Forrest), those factors influencing inmate suicide may not apply to all inmates in other jails who have attempted suicide. However, those factors need to consider when examining cases on suicidal inmates.

Secondly, the population from where the sample was taken might have resulted in selection bias because the selection procedure was voluntarily based. Some inmates were willing to participate, others were not. Therefore, this was a non-random sample in 1993.

Third, any time there are human subjects involved in research, there is great sensitivity within these institutions. When the issue is as sensitive as suicide, one can imagine the reactions of officers, jailhouse lawyers, sheriffs, and police chiefs. Reacting in a positive or negative manner will not make the problem of inmate suicide non-existent.

Fourth, because there were only 11 inmates who had attempted suicide of the 143 surveyed in 1993, this was a low probability of inmates. This does not suggest that inmate suicide had declined; rather, this number is probably higher in other jails in Mississippi and in the United States as well. As we know, Texas has the highest inmate jail suicide rate in the U.S. Thus, I am not convinced that there exist some jail suspicions that have been unsolved.

Fifth, this study was revisited in 1999. Attempts were made to collect data from the six Mississippi County Jails(i.e., Hinds, Lauderdale, Simpson, Jones, Forrest, and Alcorn) that were targeted as the sample population in the 1995 study; however, I was granted clearance into four of the six jails(i.e., Hinds County Jail, Lauderdale County Jail, Simpson County Jail and Jones County Adult Correctional Facility). Those factors influencing inmates to attempt suicide are applicable to other inmates in U.S. jails and prisons. The population from where the sample was taken did not result in selection bias because the procedure utilized was system randomization. As a result of this selection procedure, a total of 263 inmates were surveyed in which 21 had attempted suicide. The same survey was employed in the study conducted in 1999 that asked specific questions regarding actual conditions of Mississippi jails. For example, Question24a on the survey asked: Is this current jail overcrowded?" Question 24b asked, "Is this current jail deplorable?"

Finally, there has been an increased in jail and prison deaths that were results of suicide in 1999. Inmate suicide is also on the rise in private prisons and jails across the country. Human abuses that have resulted in violations of inmates rights occurred in private own jails and prisons owned by Wackenhut and Correction Corporations of America(CCA). Mississippi currently operates over 6 private jail facilities.

QUESTIONNAIRE

Please take a moment to fill out: Circle ONLY ONE Answer. The information provided is confidential and will be used for statistical purposes only.

1. What is your gender?

    A. Female

    B. Male

2. What is your race/ethnicity?

    A. African American

    B. Anglo Saxon American

    C. Latino/Hispanic American

    D. Other(please)_____

3. What is your current age?

    A. 16-19

    B. 20-23

    C. 24-27

    D. 28-31

    E. 32-35

    F. 36-39

    G. 40-43

    H. 44-47

I. 48-51

J. 52-55

K. 56-59

4. What is your present marital status?

A. Married

B. Divorced

C. Separated

D. Unmarried, living together

E. Single

F. Other____

5. Do you have any children? If yes, how many?_____

A. Yes

B. No

6. What is the highest level of education that you have obtained?

A. Less than high school(you did not graduate)

B. High school(you received your diploma)

C. Less than college(you did not graduate)

D. College graduate(you received your degree)

E. More than college(went beyond a bachelor degree)

7. Have you ever been sexually abused?

A. Yes

B. No

8. Do you have a history of alcohol abuse?

    A. Yes

    B. No

9. Do you have a history of drug abuse?

    A. Yes

    B. No

10. Have you ever had any previous arrests?

    A. Yes

    B. No

10a. If yes, how many times?

    A. 1-3times

    B. 4-6times

    C. 7-9times

    D. 10plus

11. How long have you been confined?

    A. less than 6 months

    B. 7 months-12months

    C. 13months-18months

D. 19months-24months

E. 25months-30months

F. 41months-48months

G. 49months and over

12. At the time of your arrest, were you living with your parents?

A. Yes

B. No

13. What is the present marital status of your parents?

A. Married

B. Divorced

C. Separated

D. Unmarried, living together

E. Single

F. Other_____(i.e.deceased, adopted, remarried)

14. Have you ever witnessed violence between your parents?

A. Yes

B. No

15. Were your parents ever abusive towards you?

A. Yes

B. No

16. Tell me about your family life. What was it like growing up? Describe HERE:

17. My family visits me:

    A. Less than once a week

    B. One to two times per week

    C. Once a month

    D. Three to four times a month

18. My friends visit me:

    A. Less than once a week

    B. One to two times per week

    C. Once a month

    D. Three to four times a month

19. Have you ever tried to commit suicide while incarcerated(locked up behind bars)? If yes, go to question number 20.

    A. Yes

    B. No

20 How many times?

    A. Once

    B. Twice

    C. Three times

    D. More than three times

E. Never

21. **If you thought about committing suicide while incarcerated, how did you plan to carry it out? DESCRIBE HERE:**

   A. Hanging

   B. Cutting Wrist

   C. Pill Overdose

   D. Eating Paint

   E. Other

22. **Do you know inmates who have attempted suicide while behind bars?**

   A. Yes

   B. No

22a. **If yes, how many times? If no, go to question 23.**

   A. 1-5inmates

   B. 6-11inmates

   C. 12-17inmates

   D. 18plus inmates

23. **What are some reasons why inmates commit suicide while incarcerated?**

   A. Overcrowded

   B. DeplorableConditions

   C. Isolation

   D. Lack of trained staff

E. Lack of adequate facilities

F. All of the above

G. None of the above

H. Other(specify in detail)_____

24. Have you ever been isolated from the other inmates?

A. Yes

B. No

If yes, DESCRIBE what isolation was like:

A. Lonely

B. Think

C. Peaceful

D. Boring

E. Safe

F. Other(i.e. isolated due to HIV, lockdown for fighting, horrible treated like an animal)

24a. Is this jail currently overcrowded?

A. Yes

B. No

24b. Is this jail currently deplorable(i.e. bad smell, having to consume meals close to toilet area, unclean inside jail cell, basic hygiene items denied like soap, toothpaste, meals denied)?

A. Yes

B. No

25. What is your relationship with other inmates?

   A. Very Good

   B. Fair

   C. Poor

26. How has being in jail affected you?DESCRIBE HERE:

   A. Found God

   B. Learned lesson

   C. Loss of freedom

   D. Can't see children

   E. Become more violent

   F. Lowered self-esteem

   G. Become suicidal

   H. Depression

   I. Loss of reality

   J. Loss of mental capacity

27. What offense are you charged with?

   A. Sexual Assault

   B. Murder

   C. Robbery

   D. Auto Theft

   E. Drug Offense

   F. Other_____(grand larceny, DUI, child support, shoplifting, bad
   checks, burglary, stealing gas, possession of drug paraphernalia, carjack-

ing, simple assault, public drunk, contempt of court, use of stolen credit cards, obstructing traffic, old fines, domestic violence etc..)

28. Are you awaiting trial?

A. Yes

B. No

C. Other

29. How do you feel about yourself?

A. Very Satisfied

B. Somewhat satisfied

C. Not satisfied

D. Very unsatisfied

30. How does your family feel about you?

A. They love me very much

B. They care about me

C. They accept me for who I am

D. They do not love me

31. How do you think society feels about you?

A. Cares a great deal

B. Cares somewhat

C. Cares a little

D. Does not care at all

32. Mississippi County Jails In Sample:

    A. Lauderdale County Jail

    B. Hinds County Jail

    C. Jones County Detention Correctional Adult Facility

    D. Simpson County Jail

    E. Forrest County Jail

BIBLIOGRAPHY

Books

Abbot, Allen O. 1866. *Prison Life in the South: At Richmond, Mason, Savannah, Charleston, Columbia. Charlotte, Raleigh, Goldsborough and Andersonville, During the Years 1864 and 1865.* New York, New York: Harper and Brothers.

Battin, P. Margaret. 1982. *Ethical Issues in Suicide.* Englewood Cliffs, New Jersey: Prentice-Hall, Inc.

Brent, Irving. *The Algebra of Suicides.* Los Angeles, California: Human Sciences Press, Inc.

Berk, Richard A. 1977. *Prison Reform and State Elites.* Cambridge,Massachusetts: Ballinger Publications.

Cohen, P. Neil and Gobert, J. James. 1969. *Rights of Prisoners.* Colorado Springs, Colorado: Shepard's and McGraw-Hill.

Cutler, E. James. 1969. *Lynch Law.* Montclair, New Jersey: Paterson Smith Publishing Corporation.

Grollman, A. Earl. 1988. *Suicide.* Boston, Massachusetts: Beacon Press.

Halbravaches, Maurice. 1978. *The Causes of Suicide.* New York, New York: The Free Press of McMillian Publishing Co., Inc.

Jameson, Frederic. 1972. *The Prison House of Language: A Critical Account of Structuralism and Russian Formalism.* Princeton University Press.

Johnson, Robert. 1986. *Culture and Crisis in Confinement.* Lexington, Massachusetts: D.C. Heath and Company.

Keve, Paul W. 1974. *Prison Life and Human Worth*. Minneapolis, Minnesota: University of Minnesota Press.

Lester, David. 1988. *Suicide from a Psychological Perspective*. Illinois: Charles C. Thomas.

_____. 1989. *Suicide from a Sociological Perspective*. Springfield, Illinois: Charles C. Thomas Publishers.

_____. 1992. *Why People Kill Themselves: A 1990's Summary of Research Findings on Suicidal Behavior*. Springfield, Illinois: Charles C. Thomas Publishers.

Liebling, Alison. 1992. *Suicides in Prison*. New Fetter Lane, London: Routledge, Chapman and Hall, Inc.

Maxwell, J. Atkinson. 1978. *Discovering Suicides: Studying the Social Organization of Sudden Death*. Pittsburgh, Pennsylvania: University of Pittsburgh Press.

Marx, Carl. 1993. "Correctional System in Mississippi". *Politics in Mississippi*. Salem, Wisconsin: University of Southern Mississippi.

Menninger, A. Karl. 1938. *Man Against Himself*. New York, New York: Harcourt Brace and World, Inc.

Nealy, Lisa Nikol. 1995. *Prisoners' Deaths In Local Jails: Factors Influencing Inmate Suicide*. Masters Thesis Unpublished. Jackson, Mississippi: Jackson State University Libraries.

Neese, Roberts. 1959. *Prison Exposures: With a Foreword by Elle Stanley Gardner*. Philadelphia, Chilton: Book Division.

Palmer, W. John. 1973. *Constitutional Rights of Prisoners*. Columbus, Ohio: The W.H. Anderson Company.

Peck, Dennis L. 1979. *Fatalistic Suicide*. Palo Alto, California: R and E Research Associates, Inc.

Pope, Whitney. 1976. *Durkheim's Suicide: A Classical Analyzed*. Chicago, Illinois: The University of Chicago Press.

Steward, Alva W. 1984. *Prison Overcrowding: The Problem and Suggested Solutions*. Monticello, Illinois: Vance Bibliographies.

Sylvester, Sawyer F. 1977. *Prison Homicide*. Jamaica, New York: Spectrum Publications.

Taggart, Robert. 1972. *The Prison of Unemployment: Manpower Programs for Offenders*. Baltimore: John Hopkins University Press.

Newspapers and Periodicals

Albanese, Jay S. 1983. Preventing inmate suicide. <u>Federal Probation: A Journal of Correctional Philosophy and Practice</u> Volume 47 Number 1 (March): 65-69.

Atlas, Randy. 1989. Reducing the opportunity for inmate suicide: a design guide. <u>Psychiatric Quarterly</u> 60(2): 161-171.

Bolton, Mark. 1993. Jail suicide. <u>Clarion-Ledger</u>. 16 April, Sec. 10A.

Carpenter, Lorenzo. 1992. Letter to the editor: from behind prison bars. <u>Jackson Advocate</u> 12-18 November, Sec.3A.

Franklin, J. Brad. 1992. Woman fears son will be the next prison suicide. <u>Jackson Advocate,</u> 12-18 November, Sec.1A.

Gates, Jimmy and Grace Simmons. 1992. Youth court judge calls for new detention center. <u>Clarion Ledger,</u> 10 November, Sec. 1A.

Hayes, Lindsey. 1996. Jail standards and suicide prevention:another look. <u>Jail Mental Suicide Mental Update,</u> Volume 6: 1-8.

John, Butch and Jerry Mitchell. Investigators, neshoba residents at odds in jail hanging. <u>Clarion-Ledger</u>. 16 March, Sec. 1A.

Kappeler, E. Victor and U. Rolando Carmen. 1991. Avoiding police liability for negligent failure to prevent suicide. <u>Police Chief,</u> Number 8 (August): 53-59.

Kraft, P. Beverly. 1994. Prison officials indicted. <u>The Clarion-Ledger,</u> 15 June, Sec. 1A.

Lindsey, Arnold. 1993. Small jail costly, rankin sheriff says. <u>Clarion-Ledger</u>, 29 September Sec. 1B.

Massey, L. James and Martha A. Myers. Race, labor, and punishment in postbellum georgia. <u>Social Problems</u> 38, Number 2 (May): 267-283.

Mitchell, Jerry. Rights group to examine deaths of black inmates. <u>Clarion-Ledger</u>, 12 March, Sec. 1B.

_____.1993. Study suicide prevention too, reno urged. <u>Clarion-Ledger</u>, 15 April, Sec. 1B.

_____. 1993. Jail deaths warrant probe, inspector general says. <u>Clarion-Ledger</u>, 5 May, Sec. 3B.

Simmons, Grace. 1993. Activists look into black jail deaths. <u>Clarion-Ledger</u>, 6 February, Sec. 1B.

_____. 1993. Family seeks 2nd autopsy for dead inmate. <u>Clarion-Ledger</u>, 6 February, Sec. 1B.

_____. 1993. Despite suit, say son was slain. <u>Clarion-Ledger</u>, 25 September, Sec. 1A.

_____. 1993. Students help research jail deaths. <u>Clarion-Ledger</u>, 9 April, Sec. 7A.

_____. 1994. Jail crowding: citizens want prisoners in prison. <u>Clarion-Ledger</u>, 2 June, Sec. 12A.

_____. 1994. Prison population near one million. <u>Clarion-Ledger</u>, 2 June, Sec. 7A.

_____. 1994. Prisons: lawmakers, governor on right track. <u>Clarion-Ledger</u>, 3 June, Sec. 10A.

Thornton, L.C. 1993. City jail prisoner apparently keeping promise to kill himself. <u>Clarion-Ledger</u>, 25 May, Sec. 1A.

Tisdale, Charles W. 1992. Are jailhouse suicides a new way of lynching black males? <u>Jackson Advocate</u>, 28-3 February-March, Sec. 1A.

_____.1992. Jailhouse suicide syndrome is spreading across the nation. Jackson Advocate, 5-11 November, Sec. 1A.

_____.1993. Brother says suicide victim routinely beaten. Jackson Advocate, 28-3 February-March, Sec. 1A.

_____. 1993. Focus of feds investigating into suicides question. Jackson Advocate, 20-27 May, Sec. 1A.

_____. 1993. Autopsy on hanging victim raises new questions. Jackson Advocate, 29-4 July-August, Sec. 1A.

_____. 1994. Holly enters bid to look into jail cases. Jackson Advocate, 6-12 January, Sec. 1A.

Winfree, Thomas L., and John D. Wooldredge. 1992. An aggregate-level study of inmates' suicide and deaths due to natural causes in u.s. jails. Journal of Research in Crime and Delinquency Volume 29 Number 4 (November): 460-477.

Winkler, Gregory E. 1992. Assessing and responding to suicidal jail inmates. Community Mental Health Journal Volume 28 Number 4 (August): 317-325.

Interviews

Blunston, Frank, Director of Detention Center. Interview by Lisa Nikol Nealy, 26 October 1993, Jackson, Mississippi. Personal.

Lumumba, Chokwe, Attorney. Interview by Lisa Nikol Nealy, 14 October 1993, Jackson, Mississippi. Personal.

Mayfield, Thomas, Assistant District Attorney. Interview by Lisa Nikol Nealy, 26 October 1993, Jackson, Mississippi. Personal.

McMillian, E. Malcolm, Sheriff of Hinds County. Interview by Lisa Nikol Nealy, 21 October 1993, Jackson, Mississippi. Personal.

Sollie, W.D., Chief of Police. Interview by Lisa Nikol Nealy, 28 October 1993, Meridian, Mississippi. Personal.

Sweet, Dennis, Attorney. Interview by Lisa Nikol Nealy, 13 October 1993, Jackson, Mississippi. Personal.

Quinn, W. Esther, President of National Association for Advancement of Colored People. Interview by Lisa Nikol Nealy, 8 November 1993, Jackson, Mississippi. Personal.

Public Documents

Mississippi Statistical Abstract: Division on Research, 1993.

Nie, H. Norman, et al. 1975. *SPSS Statistical Package for the Social Sciences.* New York: McGraw-Hill Book Company.

Norusis, J. Marija. 1990. *SPSS/PC Advanced Statistics 4.0.*Chicago, Illinois: SPSS, Inc.

Noruis, J. Marija. 1999. *SPSS/Base 9.0 Application Guide.* Chicago, Illinois: SPSS, Inc.

0-595-29312-3